TRUE OR FAL[SE]

1. **The best way to start a presentation** [is with a joke.] [*False!* The] audience may chuckle, but the bes... ... ... listeners that they're about to hear something that's valuable and important.
2. **The first few sentences of a presentation are crucial.** *True!* Inside find several foolproof methods for creating an opening that will grab your audience by the lapels right from the start.
3. **To get the most out of PowerPoint, you have to really know the program.** *False!* You're a businessperson, not a computer geek. Even if you know only the basics, you'll be able to use this powerful tool to wow your audience.
4. **A presentation shouldn't have "sound bites."** *False!* A well-turned phrase repeated throughout your presentation helps your audience understand and remember your message and is the linchpin of a great presentation.
5. **Telling a good story will enliven a presentation and hold the audience's attention.** *True!* But only if the story makes your message more relevant to your listeners' concerns.

PRAISE FOR *PRESENTATION S.O.S.*

"Whether you're preparing for an upcoming speech, or just want to hone your presentation skills, PRESENTATION S.O.S. offers a wealth of useful tips and sage advice on how to better connect with your audience. A practical, step-by-step guide designed to make you a more confident, dynamic, and success-ful speaker."

—MICHAEL BRUMAS, congressional staffer

"Will help professionals at any level improve their presentations."
—STERLING SANKEY, learning and organizational
executive, Bank of America

more...

"Mark Wiskup understands the risks and rewards of public speaking. In PRESENTATION S.O.S. he offers a system that will help you gain considerable confidence and self-assurance in front of an audience. The man knows his stuff!"

—JON FRIEDMAN, media columnist, Dow Jones MarketWatch

"If you're a good communicator, Mark's book will make you fantastic. If you're great, it will make you outrageous. PRESENTATION S.O.S. is a wonderful, entertaining read that is guaranteed to change the way you think and talk. It is a must-have tool that every leader needs in their tool box."

—KIM SCHEELER, president & CEO,
Tampa Chamber of Commerce

"This is the strongest book I've read on public speaking . . . Will help nervous speakers become confident and help good speakers get better. Read it before your next presentation and you'll connect with your audience with new power and strength."

—MARTY SCHAFFEL, president, Audio Visual Innovations, Inc.

"In PRESENTATION S.O.S. Mark Wiskup shares the strategies that drive great professional speakers. You can't miss if you apply these lessons."

—JO CAVENDER, West Coast president, Speakers on Healthcare, past president, International Association of Speakers Bureaus

"If we want to lead or to sell or to persuade, we must know how to make clear, compelling presentations. In PRESENTATION S.O.S., Mark Wiskup shows us how to grab and keep an audience so that it will follow or buy from or believe in us. Wiskup thoughtfully and very usefully guides us to tell stories that resonate so that the listeners not only understand but embrace the messages we're presenting. This is a must-read book for anyone who needs to 'get through' to others."

—RAFAEL PASTOR, chairman & CEO, TEC International

PRESENTATION
S.O.S.

FROM PERSPIRATION TO PERSUASION
IN 9 EASY STEPS

Mark Wiskup

WARNER
BUSINESS
BOOKS ™

NEW YORK   BOSTON

Warner Business Books
Warner Books

Time Warner Book Group
1271 Avenue of the Americas, New York, NY 10020
Visit our Web site at www.twbookmark.com.

The Warner Business Books logo is a trademark of Warner Books.

Printed in the United States of America

First Edition: September 2005

10   9   8   7   6   5   4   3   2   1

Library of Congress Cataloging-in-Publication Data

Wiskup, Mark.
   Presentation S.O.S. : from perspiration to persuasion in 9 easy steps / Mark Wiskup.—1st ed.
        p. cm.
   ISBN 0-446-69554-8
   1.   Business presentations. 2. Oral communication. 3. Public speaking. 4. Persuasion (Psychology)   I. Title: Persuasion in 9 easy steps. II. Title.
   HF5718.22.W57 2005
   658.4'52—dc22

                                                              2005010565

Book design and text composition by Meryl Sussman Levavi

This book is dedicated to the man whom thousands over the past six decades have called the best teacher they've ever had, whom I'm lucky enough to call my father, Leon A. Wiskup.

Acknowledgments

I'd like to acknowledge my agent Bob Diforio, whose efficient, calm, and straightforward professionalism quickly found this book a home at Warner Business Books, and my editor Jason Pinter, who painstakingly made my ideas stronger and more meaningful on every single page.

Finally, I'd like to acknowledge Renee Wiskup, who I'm blessed to have in my life. She's the one who swiftly puts the brakes on lousy ideas, enthusiastically encourages ideas with merit, and provides never-ending support and inspiration.

Contents

Introduction: You Are Already Moving in the
Right Direction   1

1. Fear Is a Good Thing—
   It Will Help You Become a Great Presenter   5

2. One Audience, One Power Sound Bite—
   Everybody Wins   25

3. Move Your Presentation from Good to Great:
   Learn to Tell a Story   47

4. Be Great Fast (You Can't Overcome a Lame Start)   69

5. PowerPoint Doesn't Bore Audiences,
   Lousy Speakers Do (All We Are Saying Is
   Give PowerPoint a Chance.)   93

6. Numbers Are Not Your Friends—
Use Them Sparingly 115

7. Friends Don't Let Friends Say "Basically"—
Eliminate Disconnection Expressions 133

8. Wrap Up with a Bang: Your Power Close,
Winning the Q&A Battle, and Making
the Most of the Accolades 149

9. You Are Ready to Rock: The Official Phases
of Preparation for Your Presentation 167

Conclusion 179

About the Author 181

Introduction

You Are Already Moving in the Right Direction

I know why you picked up *Presentation S.O.S.* You want to enjoy each and every opportunity you have to stand up and speak in front of others. That's a good goal. It's a challenge that you can meet. Right now you may not enjoy public speaking; rather, you may dread the very thought of facing an audience. That's okay. I see it every day in my business, and I understand how uncomfortable these feelings are. But, now you've decided you want to make a change. You want to look forward to your speaking assignment. Congratulations! By deciding to work on your presentation skills and build your confidence, you're already on your way.

Creating a powerful connection with an audience is one of the most guilt-free, indulgent pleasures that the professional world has to offer. Think of it: You can experience euphoria without any fear of a hangover. You can develop powerful relationships, filled with intensity and emotion, without using anyone and without anyone feeling used. You can pontificate, educate, proselytize, emote, influence, and receive rousing ovations after thirty minutes of it being "all about you." It can be satisfying and mood elevating, as well as a career-enhancing experience, to create a strong connection with the audience. Getting to that point of nirvana (a state of consciousness, not the Seattle rock band) will take some work and a willingness to try new ideas; however, the workload is manageable, especially when the rewards are so great. I'm going to give you instructions that are easy to follow, show examples of how to make them work, and offer lots of encouragement along the way.

The best news is you don't have to follow everything I say to reach the professional state of bliss that comes when you realize you have connected with the audience. I'm going to throw many ideas at you. You may find that some of them don't fit your style, or you may think they just won't work. (For example, I ask you not to "thank" the audience at the beginning of your presentation. I'll give you something better to say.) That's just fine. By considering new ideas and playing with different communication styles you haven't considered before, you'll gain confidence and better podium skills.

I believe there is no such thing as a perfect presenter. There are those presenters who click with the audience, and those who don't. There are presenters who have confidence they'll have a good experience when they stand in front of others, and there are those who can't imagine it being anything less than pure unadulterated torture.

My goal is to move you from the feelings of dread, if that's where you are, to feelings of excited anticipation for your next presentation. I've based all of these lessons, tips, and examples on my experiences as a broadcast journalist, media production company entrepreneur, and presentation skills coach. No research, studies, or data were harmed or even consulted in the creation of this book. I'm going to tell you exactly what I see working successfully with my clients every day.

If possible, read the chapters in order, because they build upon each other. There's no tragedy if you don't. For example, skip to chapter 5 if you're dying to make the most of PowerPoint skills in your next presentation, and then go back and pick up the rest. The chapters are meant to follow one another, but each has value by itself.

I know you might be a little frightened to begin the process of getting comfortable in front of an audience. If so, chapter 1 is the perfect place to start.

1

Fear Is a Good Thing—It Will Help You Become a Great Presenter

WHAT YOU WILL LEARN FROM THIS CHAPTER:

- It is healthy and reasonable to be fearful of your upcoming presentation.
- The reasons why your fears are well founded.
- How to use your fears to create a great presentation.

It's going to be okay! I know you are nervous about your next presentation, and that is understandable. I also say it's good. Being nervous will give you the energy you need to create a vibrant talk and then deliver it to your audience with power and confidence. The fact that your upcoming presentation is giving you a case of the willies is a good sign. It shows you care. It shows you want to be good, and improve. Please don't wish for the jitters to go away! Accomplished speakers, like athletes and entertainers, recognize that sense of discomfort is a tool to help them focus, prepare thoroughly, and perform well. The physiological distress signals your body sends out to stop you from taking the podium—sweaty palms (as well as upper lips, foreheads, and underarms), constricted throat, butterflies in the stomach, shortness of breath—come from realistic fears. Good. In fact, as my kids say, "It's all good."

Your body is telling you, "You're in for a fight." Get ready. This anxiety can be channeled to help you heighten your senses, intellect, creativity, and drive. Deliver a powerful performance, receive encouragement and insightful questions from the audience, and you've jumped a major hurdle: You've kicked a little tail on those presentation fears.

I don't want to talk you out of your fear. I'm not going to tell you not to worry about your next presentation. Your anxiety shows me you're perceptive, not paranoid. You understand that when you stand in front of an audience, every single face hides a fair-weather fan. You *can* get those in the audience to become fans and cheer for you, your ideas, and your proposals. All you have to do is create a strong connection with every one of them, no matter how big the room is. You can do it, and understanding and accepting your fear is the first step. The worst presenters, I believe, are the ones with no fear, no sweat. They think they're already pretty good and don't care about improving the impact of their presentation on the audience.

The comic dying onstage always says, "Wow, tough crowd." I say they're all tough. From the PTA parents in cafeterias to the corporate "C-levels" (MBA marketing lingo for CEOs, COOs, CIOs, and CFOs) in mahogany conference rooms, to the colleagues you hang out with every day in the coffee room, every audience is demanding. They expect the speaker to be good, even if you're their "bud," "sister," "bro," or the only one in the office they can talk to about the suspense behind last night's eviction ceremony on *Big Brother Five.*

Audiences don't like being disappointed. They will quickly turn on any speaker who's not building a connection. Therefore, the task ahead is easy. When the spotlight is on you, never let the audience down and you'll be golden. It's a good goal—one you can reach.

I can say, after years of sitting in them and talking to them, that audiences are not unfair. But they are quick to judge. Once you understand how to connect with the audience members, you'll find you can please them every time. Audiences will keep buying what you're selling as long as they think they want and need your ideas, your insights, and your thoughts. They are the ultimate conspicuous consumers, right out of Thorstein

Veblen's *Theory of the Leisure Class* (wow, Dad, five years of college wasn't down the drain!). They will cheer you and keep buying your thoughts as long as you please them. Keep pleasing them, and you'll keep the boo birds at bay, forever.

That's a good ambition because a disparaging audience won't actually boo you to your face if you bore them. Boos might be more helpful than what really happens because instead, they'll do worse. They will cruelly mock you behind your back if you fail to connect with them. For the next fifteen to thirty minutes, they want you to rock their world. And they expect you to know how to do it. After all, there *you* are, in front of everybody, commanding all the attention.

So your fears are well placed. I guarantee they will not "love you for just being you," as your mom told you while wiping away your tears on the way to the first day at a new elementary school. The audience is filled with professional adults who will only "love you" if you connect with them, inform them, and help them. Follow the right steps and you can do all three every time.

If you're a week away from the presentation and your palms are starting to sweat, know that you're in good company. Everyone who has to stand in front of others, in the figurative spotlight, begins with these same fears. Those who succeed will embrace the fears, akin to that famous Hollywood stereotype: the vacant, unemployed blond-haired surfer assessing ferocious fifteen-foot swells that crest and violently pound the shore. The tanned and seemingly inarticulate surfer gazes intently at the threatening horizon and says directly to the waves, "Come on, dude, let's party!"

That's how confident and successful speakers feel, imagining the faces in the audience they'll be standing in front of in an hour or a week. The real pros fully understand this is treacherous professional territory. They understand it can cause embarrassment and pain, and might even "leave a mark" on their careers as well as their psyches. They also know fear creates realizations that will enable them to perform well, navigate the punishing environment, and bring them a rewarding and exhilarating experience that our character out of Malibu central casting would describe as "totally righteous."

Your fear is good. No one should talk you out of it. And they'll try. Heavens yes, they'll stick their noses right in the middle of your fears. Who hasn't experienced that surreal scene that could have come out of *Ozzie and Harriet, Father Knows Best,* or *The Brady Bunch*? Here's how it goes in case you haven't had the pleasure:

You're going over your notes at your desk. You're feeling tense because your presentation is tomorrow. Enter the forever-patronizing Mike Brady character (Mike being the natural father of Greg, Bobby, and Peter) in your life. With a gentle wave of the hand and head tilted in full condescension mode, he says, "I know you're nervous. But here's a little trick that always works. Just pretend everyone in the audience is in their underwear and you'll be fine." As my daughter says, "Eeeoow! Gross!"

How is this underwear thing supposed to help? It's cruel. Well intentioned, but cruel nonetheless. It may be disturbing and even slightly sickening to envision your peers, your customers, your bosses in matching sets of Hanes, but it's not calming to a jumpy speaker. Only in the bizarre alternative universe of sitcoms does the "underwear" advice assuage the dread of the next presentation, transforming an anxious frown into a smile of earnest enthusiasm and confidence. That probably didn't help you in high school and it's not going to help you now. "They" are wrong. There *is* something to fret about. And it's real! I want to take a look at your biggest fears, show you why they aren't imagined, and prove that is the first step to overcome in your meaningful and connecting presentation.

It's worth the effort. You may never bring yourself to say, "Come on, dude, let's party," as you step to the podium, but you'll be more confident at the front of the room as you open you mouth to speak.

Presentation Fear #1: The Audience Will Judge Me Because I'm Taking Up Their Valuable Time

You're right. They will. Take their time and you're taking something from them they'll never get back. That's why audiences are brutal. It's not that audiences set out to be unkind. Bad speakers force the harsh judgments, barely stifled anger, unpleasant thoughts, and lack of compassion a disgruntled audience tends to spit out. I don't have sympathy for a speaker who is professionally "falling and can't get up" during a failing presentation. I say the bad karma is well deserved. The speaker didn't prepare enough, one way or the other. Lousy presenters are thieves; they steal time.

Audiences are investing their most valuable asset in you.

They're giving you a chunk of their lives. And they expect return on that investment. They expect to be better off after giving you fifteen to thirty minutes of their time. Everybody expects to gain after spending something: money on that new top from Abercrombie & Fitch, that new ionic freshener from the Sharper Image (how many different models of ionic air fresheners are there anyway?), or their time listening to you. They want return on their money, their time, their investment. They don't expect a huge return. A few new ideas, something that will help them—delivered in a pleasant way—is all they ask. And so many times they get ripped off. No return on the investment, and even worse, the principal is gone. Thirty minutes of their life they will never get back. And there is no return policy.

On top of that, this all takes place in a closed conference room environment that is not an exercise in democracy. It's a dictatorship. For a short time, you're the omnipotent overlord of the room, whether or not you want to be. You're spewing forth information, and the audience members have no choice but to let it spill over them, and perhaps soak it in. Everyone accepts this premise. It's what a presentation scenario is. The audience members for your upcoming talk will accept it. You accept it when you're in the audience for the speaker who follows you. We all have learned to accept a dictator at the front of the room. We all will keep doing so as long at the rule is pleasing to us.

The core of a presentation tableau lies in the fact that for it to work, everyone in the room must stop conversing so you can talk. Not just for a minute or two, like cocktail party conversations, but for fifteen to thirty minutes. For that period, you're not only the center of your universe; you're the center of theirs. They're stuck listening to you, and the rules of social decency mandate they have to at least act like they're listening.

It's a false dictatorship, though, and here's the nerve-racking part. The speaker doesn't have the real power, the audience does. That's why your stomach churns more and more as the presentation looms ever closer. You are in danger of a riotous corporate rebellion in the mind of every audience member, from the moment you as the "pseudo-dictator" assume a very tenuous control of the room.

If you're engaging, helpful, and fun to listen to, audience members won't mind delivering their power to you. They'll know you're the boss. As long as you connect, the audience will suffer your false dictatorship gladly, not minding at all that you're doing all the talking. If they like the way you handle your power, they'll ask you to talk again soon. That's a clear indication that they've enjoyed your pseudo-authoritative rule, and that they want to experience it again. A happy, pleased audience tells you they're better off when you're talking and they're listening.

Even the question-and-answer period is autocratic. The speaker decides who to call on and who will respond.

Once you stop connecting, you're not such a benevolent dictator. The audience will view you as abusive. They'll start to rebel. It will get ugly, quickly, and you may not even sense it until it is too late. They will think unkind thoughts, say unkind words afterward, and hope you never rise to power in the room again.

They'll even start to plot against you and your time-wasting efforts. A lackluster presentation or two and you'll realize you never really had any power when you stood at the podium. It's no fun when the rabble is rousing. Keep them connected and you can quell the mob into dutiful, pleasant submission. It's what the audience wants. It's what I think when I sit in an audience. I will gladly give my time and attention to a speaker who is enjoyable to listen to and who teaches me something.

> Realization #1:
> The audience will judge you positively
> if you add to their day.

Presentation Fear #2: The Audience Members Will Not Listen to Me—They Have Been Burned by Other Speakers

This fear is about facing an audience filled with broken presentation hearts. We all have that bright and witty, yet bitter, caustic, and forlorn, friend who keeps experiencing miserable luck in romance. We're always saying that friend is, "really a sweet person down deep." Friends like this never go into a first date with giddy, joyful anticipation. Rather, they are jaded, sardonically expecting the worst. They tell you it will probably be a wretched time, and the only redeeming feature will be providing you with some laughs the next day about another jerk, another beast, or another loser. They always say they really just want romance and someone they can really talk to. Why the gloom?

The pessimism and sarcasm come from bad experiences. They've been misled, cheated on, and unceremoniously dumped, when all they've been is open, honest, accepting, and giving. They've been hurt.

That's exactly how audiences feel. They want great conference room experiences, but alas, they keep coming up professionally empty! They are quietly suspicious of every speaker who stands in front of them. They too have been hurt, misled, and burned (tear!) time and time again by speakers they'd hoped would be enriching, but instead turned out to be insincere and a waste of time. That's why they're suspicious of you, even though you're just now making your way to the mike and haven't even begun to talk.

I know that's how you and I feel when we are in the audience. "Will this be good, or lousy? Will this be a waste of my time? Oh, this won't be good, I just know it! I wish I was back in my office, doing work I really need to get done. Why did I agree to take this meeting?" Your judgments are unfair, but they come from your unfortunate experience, not unfounded insecurities.

Now the tables are turned. You know when you step to the front of the room; all those attentive and sometimes encouraging pairs of eyes mask caustic and ruthless snap-judgment mechanisms—the same kind you make. They're giving you a grade on everything you do. It's as if your critical first-quarter production or marketing presentation in the conference room is some type of freakish corporate Miss America pageant. Audiences never reward just a good effort or hard work. You have to win them over every time. They're ready to mentally record with a searing red marker your performance score in all kinds of categories and competitions from the moment you open your mouth until the moment you take your seat.

You know this all too well. You know the audience members can and will be mean and unforgiving, all the while politely clapping and facetiously chuckling at the lame humor coming from the speaker. You know about the forced smiles hiding clinched lips whispering the evaluation, "This guy is a moron." You know this because sometimes that smile and those unkind words have come from you. That's right. I'm alleging you've been a mean-spirited and unforgiving member yourself. I know I have been and I will continue to be. I argue that everyone, who's not a parent or child of the speaker, becomes grumpy at warp speed after just ten minutes of a lousy presentation.

This is all good! It's frightening, perhaps, but good. Realizing the audience is suspicious is the first step to winning and rewarding their confidence. Help them to trust again (another tear, this time of joy), and they'll clap enthusiastically and mean it. They'll be telling others at coffee the next day how professionally "hot" you are. Connect with the audience and you break the chain of presentation distrust and heartache.

Realization #2: The audience will forget
they've been burned as soon as you give
them a good experience.

Presentation Fear #3: The Audience Will Tune Me Out

If you make a connection with the audience, they will not tune you out. If you make good on the investment they're making in you, they will stick with you. It's the law (I just made up) of presentation macroeconomics: Audiences keep investing when they keep getting a return.

Like that guy in the gym says, the one who's spotting you on the bench press and yelling encouragement as your face turns beet red on the twelfth rep when you really were done at eleven: "It's all you, man, I mean, I'm not doin' nuthin'! Come on, man, one more. It's all you." Your relationship with the audience, your connection and disconnection, is all about you, nothing else. It is, as the guy yells, "all you, man!" Your presentation success depends on you alone, and you alone can succeed, every time. But first you have to stop worrying about all the overblown concerns regarding short attention spans.

Please, avoid that trap of convincing yourself that audience members are incapable of listening to important ideas (your important ideas, gall dernit) because of the ubiquity of high-speed Internet, DirecTV, the iPod, *Total Request Live,* and Xbox. When you believe that, you sound pitiful and old, longing for the days of the three network stations and one independent you got from the antenna on the roof, long before all this digital-highway crap. You know, back when people could really listen. Back when people would really talk about ideas. Say that, and I believe you're fooling yourself into thinking you don't have control of your presentation. You *have* all the control. You can be great, and the proliferation of DSL lines and wireless Internet connections cannot stop you!

I get cranky when I hear cocktail chatter alleging our collective attention spans are getting shorter every year. I'm not a sociologist, audiologist, neurologist, or anything that requires an understanding of even simple physiology or a state certification. Consequently, I'm not basing my massive skepticism on any research I've done or facts I've studied. I see plenty of non-research-based evidence around me every day that convinces me digital media is not to blame for the fact that "we just don't pay attention to anything anymore." I say we all pay attention to things we find rewarding. Believing otherwise is a cop-out.

Blaming technology for shorter attention spans is like the guy who's convinced his girlfriend won't accept his marriage proposal because she is "afraid of commitment." She's not "afraid of commitment." She is, however, "afraid of commitment" to him. We still pay attention to what's important, no matter how many channels are on the cable box or satellite dish. All of us pay attention to things longer than a *Real World* swish pan from one arguing college kid to another if we feel it a good investment of our time.

I've never seen parents at a dance recital zoning out, reading a book, or chatting on a cell phone when their five-year-old daughter is performing her first pirouette onstage. I've never heard a parent seated in the splintery bleachers at the ball field say, "Oh wow, my son Chris is in the on-deck circle. I'll just keep reading today's *Wall Street Journal.* Besides, Chris will be up again in a few innings."

I say our attention spans are not shorter. Don't worry that the audience is too media/message overwhelmed to listen to you. Every single one of us will pay attention, for long periods of time, when we believe there's something worth paying attention to. If your kid is onstage, you are mesmerized. If a musical performance connects with you, you're disappointed when the lights come up. *Titanic* was longer than *Gigli* and *Dude, Where's My Car?* put together, and that didn't stop a record number of patrons from seeing it over and over again.

It you're good at the microphone, the audience will pay attention, regardless of how many digital, print, broadcast, and billboard messages have bombarded them that day. If you're lousy, they may dismiss you and you won't even know it. And they'll be good at hiding their feelings. Oh sure, they may be looking right at you. Maybe they're even making eye contact. But they're not paying attention. It's a facetious exercise. The audience may be smiling and nodding, but zoning out, going somewhere else.

Where on earth can they be heading off to? Now that you've disconnected with them, they're going anywhere their minds can take them to get away from you: their picks in the upcoming fantasy football draft, bargains in the shoe department at the semiannual sale at Nordstrom, calorie math (if they work out this afternoon will that make up for that fourth Margarita last night?), that pesky dog leg on the par-five seventeenth hole, what's for lunch, what's for dinner, what's going on with Paris Hilton? They'll think of anything to tune you out.

Your fear of them tuning you out is real. Use that as motivation to create a brisk, fun-to-listen-to, and meaningful presentation, which will provide them with a great return on the investment of their time. You can blame MTV for a lot of unfortunate things (the rise of Duran Duran in the '80s, Hanson in the '90s, and those irritating boy bands), but not for the audience's losing interest in your idea. You control that yourself.

> Realization #3: The audience will not
> tune you out if you make it impossible
> for them to do so.

Presentation Fear #4: The Audience Will Not Like Me, Because I Will Make Mistakes

This is a fear that is just not realistic. You'll make mistakes. Guess what? I say the audience won't care and probably won't remember. Your slight miscues never matter to the audience a fraction of how much they matter to you. But I understand this anxiety. They're expecting greatness but are conditioned for mediocrity. You worry that if you deliver anything short of a superior presentation, they will tune you out and then blast you at the coffee machine later in the day. There are no ties in this game. Either you win them over, or you lose.

"Great," say the fretting speakers, "I just have to be perfect every minute, every time." I disagree. Audiences don't expect perfection and they won't give you credit for it. So, please try to forget about it. I say audiences are both sympathetic and forgiving. They pride themselves on being very magnanimous and understanding. So much so, they enjoy seeing a misstep from the speaker. They just don't want it to last too long, to be completely inappropriate, or to be gross.

So go ahead, get something stuck in your throat for a second or two. Start to cough. Lose your place for a moment. Say "billion" when you meant "million." But stay cool, don't draw attention to it, and move on. When you find your place after shuffling through the order of your notes for a second or two, the members of the audience give themselves a silent and self-congratulatory mental pat on the back, "Well, I was pulling for her. I knew she'd be okay." Audiences love an underdog, as long as the underdog becomes a winner quickly. They'll turn away in horror from any train wreck at the podium. So don't scream, "I'm so stuuuuupid. That's million, not billion, moron! Ach, I'm so lame, so clueless, such a loser." This type of self-flagellation makes everyone uncomfortable, so rein it in.

The audience doesn't want or expect perfect. It's never a good goal for a speaker. You can easily dump the fear of having to be perfect. It's not realistic and it is not important.

Realization #4: The audience accepts
mistakes and will not hold them against you.

Presentation Fear #5: The Audience Will Dismiss My Ideas, and Me

This is a tough one that I can't dismiss. The fear of being tagged a lightweight is the heaviest of the fears. It's reasonable, and just like the other fears, very real. Adults don't usually belittle each other with the harsh stereotypes of their adolescent years: "loser," "geek," "dumb jock," "brainiac." Adults use much more refined put-downs that are just as devastating: "lightweight," "lacking in bandwidth," "empty suit," "off-point," "unprepared," or the worst comment: "irrelevant."

The fear of being dismissed means that you've accepted the previous fears and have even overcome them. Great! It means that you're worried the audience will judge your performance and your ideas on their own merit, ignoring their past prejudices. Your focus now is on *your* work, *your* thoughts, *your* vision, *your* analysis, *your* intellect, and *your* drive.

This is the best fear for you as you prepare for your next talk. It's the fear of not being taken seriously. It's the fear the audience will accuse you of "not knowing what you're talking about." There is no worse professional criticism, and it's something to be frightened about. It will also push you to build your presentation in such a way that the audience will respect your ideas and your thoughts, even if they'll never agree with them. That's a big win for every presentation.

The first step to becoming relevant is to make sure you're making a connection with the audience for every idea with which you take up their time. If the audience is still in the room with you, understanding and then considering your thoughts, they're not dismissing them. They may not agree with your ideas, but they will listen and they will give you your due. That's a victory for your professional standing, even more so when you conquer this significant fear.

Realization #5: When you build a connection
with the audience for every idea,
the audience will respect you.

You're not freaking out "for no good reason." Your reasons are sound. So, now, I ask you to stop freaking out. You are normal and you can and will get over it.

The result is that something remarkable will happen to your deep, dark, constricting fears. But don't get too hopeful. They won't go away. They can't and shouldn't. But their paralyzing sharpness and impact will fade. You'll still hear those fears, whispering in the background. Only now, you've got a pillow over your ears. You know about the fears, and they won't bother you.

Action items for your next presentation:

1. Understand that the audience will judge you because you're taking up their valuable time. You must figure out how to make good on their investment in you.

2. Understand that the audience is jaded and has been burned by other speakers. Vow to help them "learn to love again!" (Sniffle, tear.)

3. Understand you've got a battle to gain the focus of the minds behind every set of eyes in front of you. Know it's a battle you can and will win.

4. Realize perfection is not the goal. Nobody cares. A few stumbles don't matter, nor will they be remembered. A

good or a bad presentation is never influenced by a few missteps.

5. Face the fact you will be judged on the strength of the presentation of your ideas. Present your ideas in a way that will be compelling, and you will be respected. Not always agreed with, but always taken seriously.

2

One Audience, One Power Sound Bite— Everybody Wins

WHAT YOU WILL LEARN FROM THIS CHAPTER:

- Why you need a power sound bite to connect with your audience.
- How to develop a power sound bite for your next presentation.
- How to create supporting statements for your power sound bite.

You are tough, strong, and determined. You are now staring the phobias of your upcoming presentation in the face. Let's beat them back. The power sound bite (PSB) provides a winning, clear, and definitive reason for you to be at the front of the room, commanding the attention of others in front of you. This lesson will teach you to develop that powerful, concise, and, most of all, memorable statement to guide the audience through your presentation, which will knock your fears down so they can't get up.

When you have a strong PSB in your hand and on your lips, you have the solid foundation for a memorable presentation. Most presentations that are dubbed "lousy," "boring," or "a real snore fest" are because the speaker hasn't crafted and supported a PSB. The "snore fest" speakers are inconsiderate, throwing a bunch of undisciplined information at the audience, certain in the knowledge it will all add up to a brilliant conclusion. I say it doesn't. The audience needs and wants to be steered. That's the critical part of their connection to you, the speaker. Lead them with a memorable PSB that you will repeat throughout your presentation, and you will maintain a solid connection to your audience.

Some people show a haughty disrespect for any combination of the words "sound" and "bite." Let's deal with their misdirected communication snobbery and then move on to helping you create a power sound bite for your next presentation. "They" (you know them) say we live in a sound-bite world. They

27

accompany that assessment with a look of disdain and of having detected a whiff of foulness in the air, like there's something wrong with sound-bite communication. They also act like it's a recent aberration. Boy, are they wrong.

Sound bites aren't bad and they are not new. I also say we should be thankful that the best speakers throughout time have honed their messages. We're all better off for it. The audience for your upcoming presentation will be, too, if you follow suit. I believe a lone, ringing, clear sound bite or quotable main idea is the basis of all strong presentations. Let's take a look at three different familiar sound bites, delivered decades apart. Each sound bite gave its speaker a tremendous connection to his respective audience.

Franklin Roosevelt knew this in March 1933 when he addressed Americans in his inaugural speech. It was the Depression, and Americans were experiencing a frightening economic slump that threatened them with job insecurity, meager paychecks, and poverty—even the loss of basic food and shelter. After hearing FDR's inaugural speech, most Americans went to sleep that night believing "the only thing we have to fear is fear itself." Even though the speech ran almost twenty minutes, Americans specifically remembered "the only thing we have to fear is fear itself." It stuck with them for several years as the country pulled itself out of a devastating depression. We still remember that single, clear, inspiring idea more than seventy years later. Roosevelt created a positive, thoughtful, and easy-to-remember quote while delivering a message of hope, asking Americans to abandon their paralysis and fear.

Martin Luther King Jr. delivered perhaps the single most profound line of the electronic age on the steps of the Lincoln Memorial in August of 1963. Amid social strife and cultural upheaval he told the country of his unbounded optimism, which still sends a poignant shiver down the spine and creates moist eyes. He said, "I have a dream." It was a brilliant, simple, single idea that punctuated a three-thousand-word address over and over again. His dream was not about his personal wishes, but about the dramatic verbal snapshots of a peaceful, kind, and just America that would benefit all. His dream that the future could be bright and tranquil, replacing the current misery founded in the inequities of the past, became the rallying sound bite for decency battles across the globe.

In the one and only debate of the 1980 presidential campaign, Ronald Reagan's searing response to Jimmy Carter's defense of his presidency boiled down to a rhetorical question as he addressed the American people: "Are you better off than you were four years ago?" Reagan counted on this one sound bite (with the unspoken, but implied "no!") ringing in the ears of Americans as they went to the polls just eight days later. Many credit this subtle-yet-biting power sound bite's scoff at the unimpressiveness of the status quo with having influenced unsure voters and delivering the White House to the Republicans. Reagan had an entire detailed agenda for the changes he would make, but he focused on convincing voters that the Carter administration had been ineffective. He sculpted that agenda to one precise rhetorical question, and he won. Compared with the aggressive, hostile, and mean-spirited attacks we've seen in many races since then, the simple and almost gentle approach seems elegant and dignified.

These different presentations at three distinct points in time, with three different purposes, all share a similar foundation. They use what I'm calling a "power sound bite" as a foundation of their main ideas. Power sound bite is my contemporary description of what speech teachers may call a central theme. We're all talking about the same thing: When you're standing in front of people, give them a strong sentence or two to keep them focused and remembering what you said as they leave the room and when they wake up tomorrow.

When you center your presentation on a PSB, you're doing a lot to dispel the mistrust and foreboding that both you and the audience face as you step to the podium. Your power sound bite will show the audience a great deal. It shows you want your presentation to be a positive experience for the audience. It demonstrates that you are respectful, creating an easy-to-follow presentation that is never patronizing. Your unifying memorable thought, your power sound bite, allows you to create an instant connection with the audience, eliminating their natural distrust. Remember (tear!), they've been burned before. With a winning PSB in hand as you step to the front of the room for your next presentation, you're already beating back the fears presented in chapter 1.

Flashback time: As someone who proudly camped out in front of Ticketmaster locations to secure a good seat for the Rolling Stones, The Who, Led Zeppelin, and David Bowie, I can't claim to be a fan of the one-hit-wonder Baha Men. I do admit, however painfully, that several years ago I had "Who Let the Dogs Out" in my head and couldn't get it out. Even now and then, it still creeps back in. You may not be a fan of reality shows, but please admit, "The tribe has spoken," and "You're fired," have become ever-present catch phrases. They are great power sound bites!

From William Shakespeare's "To be, or not to be," to Sally Field's "You like me, you really like me!" sound bites in many forms create memorable moments that last a long time. You and I may never play a tragic hero or be a reality show guru or Academy Award winner. Just learn from those guys: Definitive "hooks," images, and sound bites are sometimes the only memories that linger for more than twenty-four hours. That's the way it's always been, and the way it always will be. We've always lived in a sound-bite world. Katie Couric didn't create it. Walter Cronkite didn't create it. Jay Leno didn't create it. Edward R. Murrow didn't create it. Marie Antoinette may have never said, "Let them eat cake," but someone in the streets of Paris who created the rumor understood how much havoc a negative sound bite can wreak.

Power sound bites are what make the oral traditions of all cultures work. Sound bites are as necessary and helpful (and possibly hurtful) today as they were even before DirecTV and picture cell phones. Your PSB is critical to the success of your next talk. Embrace this critical starting point and you're already beginning the process of connecting with an audience. You can create a winning power sound bite for every presentation.

The first task is to conquer all the preparation fears we went over in chapter 1 to develop and hone that power sound bite for your next audience. I hope to convince you this is essential. It's your presentation bedrock. You need a PSB to create a blueprint for your presentation that you and the audience will keep referring to. When you deliver that power sound bite with confidence, it bathes the room in comfort and creates instant good vibrations. The audience won't necessarily agree with your power sound bite. That doesn't matter, because you shouldn't be expecting total agreement in every presentation. Instead, your goal should be to connect with the audience, gain their respect and careful consideration.

That's the first step to getting the audience members to move to your side. That's why the best presenters spend a good bulk of their preparation time on creating their power sound bite. They know the math: One PSB for every presentation equals one audience that will remember and even act on that power sound bite. Once you've developed your power sound bite, it's much easier to figure out the rest of what you're going to say.

Let's get to it. You can develop a power sound bite for every presentation by asking and then answering these two questions:

- What single idea do I want the audience repeating as they leave the room?
- What single idea do I want them repeating to their friends and colleagues the next day?

Keep it to one idea, not three or six. No one wants to sort through the five absolutely critical ideas ringing in their ears as they leave the room. No one at the coffee machine the next day will be able to repeat your six distinct themes. But they will remember and be able to repeat one strong power sound bite. Please, don't ask the audience to concentrate on three or four or five PSBs. That's asking too much. Why should they work that hard? You aren't that great (don't be mad, nobody is) and they won't. Everybody sitting in front of you has had a demanding enough day without having to work to understand your multiple, competing, and perhaps confusing ideas. They want one idea, and they want you to build a case for that idea. A single power sound bite that you repeat and support is the best way to maintain your contact with the audience, no matter how much they want to drift to their fantasy football picks.

Your topic may be complex. Good presenters love complex topics. Their job is to make it easy for the audience to care about their perspective on that complex issue. When you make it easy for them to care, you make it easy for them to focus. That's why I want you to work to get it to one power sound bite and make it come alive for your audience.

Now, you may be saying, "Well, heck, I can't dumb this down to one main idea. I mean (pick one that might fit for you: casualty insurance options, multidisciplinary curriculum issues, investment strategies, marketing plans, manufacturing productivity, changes in employment law, etc.) are a heck of a lot more complicated than that." You're right, and so am I. Put your work into making that complex topic center around a single unifying PSB and you're on the way to becoming the type of presenter audiences look forward to listening to. Your topic isn't more taxing or complicated than the assignments faced by

Franklin Roosevelt, Martin Luther King Jr., or Ronald Reagan. You're not trying to pull the country out of the Depression, create an equal society, or become the leader of the free world. Those speakers understood that the more complex and contentious the issue, the more the audience welcomes clarity of a single unifying sound bite. Your job, as the speaker and dictator of the room, is to deliver a strong power sound bite to your listening subjects. If you don't go to the trouble of creating, supporting, and repeating your PSB, you're putting a target on your back and setting yourself up for some vicious coffee room criticism from your colleagues.

Most speakers you've found boring refuse to do the hour or so of heavy lifting it takes to build a power sound bite. The men and women at the microphone who have you glassy eyed and fighting off sleep, or playing "rock-paper-scissors" with the guy next to you, all have the same thing in common. They think the best way to help the audience understand the topic is by reciting as many facts as possible. They are under the mistaken impression that the greater the number of ideas they spit out, the more impressive the performance. These misled speakers imagine the audience walking out in the foyer after their "complete" presentation and saying, "Wow, that was thorough. It was crammed full of so many different competing ideas and themes, I lost count. Now that was a memorable speech." What the audience is actually saying is, "That was a half hour of my life I'll never get back. What was he talking about anyway? I'm hungry, where are the croissants?" You can always avoid this scenario when you dedicate the time and energy to creating your power sound bite.

You can do this in the same amount of time it takes for the guys on *Law & Order* to discover a body, find a suspect, and hold a trial: about sixty minutes. You're making a great investment by taking that hour and focusing on the thirty to sixty minutes it will take to get some ideas down on paper. Pour some sweat equity into that PSB and your investment will keep paying you back during every moment of your presentation. You never feel an intense workout at the gym or a long brisk walk was a waste of time. You feel healthy and strong and that you used your time well. Developing your power sound bite gives you that same sense of personal satisfaction, maybe a little glow!

So let's get down to business, and the steps to creating your power sound bite. You will be able to do this. Everyone I work with and coach has had tremendous success creating PSBs once they know how. It merely takes an understanding of what to do and the discipline to do it. I'll give you the first one (understanding) and cheer you on for the second (discipline). The speakers who connect with the audience by delivering a power sound bite during every presentation are no more brilliant than you are. They just have something you don't have. They have memorized the rules and procedures for creating memorable power sound bites. Now you're going to have them too! Follow these guidelines and you will hear the audience repeating your words as they leave the room. That's a great feeling. It chases the fears presented in chapter 1 even farther away.

Your power sound bite does not have to be catchy, bouncy, or clever. That's for politicians and comedians. Your PSB may be as many as three or four sentences. This is an exercise in creating a connection with the audience and becoming memorable, not creating a slogan or a lyrical hook in a song. Power sound bites work best when they're thoughtful, respectful, and real. Let's go through the rules you'll need to start drafting your PSB.

Make Your Power Sound Bite About the Audience

Audiences want you to talk about them. They will listen to your ideas, as long as you're working to show them how your ideas will help, impact, or affect *them*. The best way to do that is to have the power sound bite address the audience directly. Remember, they're not sitting there to pay homage to you. They are sitting in front of you and hoping you'll make their tasks, their assignments, and their lives better. To fulfill this promise, consider demonstrating in the most compelling and inspiring way possible that your ideas are not just good in general, not just ideas you like, but ideas that are meant for them.

♦ Strong power sound bite example: *You are the best team in the region. You are the ones who will show everyone else how to achieve superior results. I'm delighted and honored to lead you in your efforts.*

♦ Weak power sound bite example: *My goal is to make our team number one in the region. No matter what it takes, we're going to get there. As your leader, I'll make sure of it.*

Critique: The strong power sound bite is about the audience. The weak power sound bite is about the speaker.

Your Power Sound Bite Should Be Direct, Strong, and Simple

Great, winning power sound bites take a strong stand. Remember, the audience has coughed up their time to you. They want intensity and thoughtful ideas, even if they wind up disagreeing with you. It's okay to tell the audience that you are undecided about an important issue. Just develop a power sound bite that is strong and definitive about why you're still on the fence. Audiences are drawn to strong, thoughtful, and direct statements that address their concerns.

- Strong power sound-bite example: *When you support these goals for the direction of our marketing efforts, you'll be assuring a good, profitable year for the company, making your customers happy, and putting more money in your wallet.*
- Weak power sound-bite example: *I'm sure after you hear all the facts in my presentation, you'll come to the correct decision about my goals for the direction of our marketing efforts.*

Critique: The strong power sound bite is direct and positive. The weak PSB contains the words "I'm sure you'll come to the correct decision," which is vague and patronizing.

Your Power Sound Bite Should Be Offensive, Never Defensive

Defensive tones are not helpful to your power sound bite. They can hurt you with the audience, no matter how much indignation you swaddle around it. This is true even when you're being attacked, and the purpose of your presentation is to defend yourself. Be aggressive, be strong, be indignant, but be positive. Defensive sound bites never sound good in the room, the next day, or the next decade.

We've learned this lesson from two U.S. presidents: Richard Nixon ("I'm not a crook") and Bill Clinton ("I did not have sexual relations with that woman"). These negative and defensive sound bites still create amusement, chuckles, and fodder for satirical abuse. When you're defensive, you create ammunition for your critics. You are creating a power sound bite that hurts you! After all, the defensive words did come out of your mouth.

President Clinton has another minor entry in the defensive power sound bite hall of fame with the now comic concession, "I didn't inhale." It wasn't the theme of his presentation at that news conference in 1992, but even the most ardent Clinton supporters and apologists admit it has become laughably memorable.

- ◆ Strong power sound-bite example: *Our team has done a great job on the production floor to meet all of our customers' needs, despite a wide variety of obstacles and a lack of support from our colleagues. We will continue to succeed.*
- ◆ Weak power sound-bite example: *I do not accept the claim*

by our sales department that we are letting the company down. We are not in the business of disappointing our customers.

Critique: The strong power sound bite is positive and uplifting. The weak PSB casts pallor with the words "letting the company down."

Power Sound Bites Ask for a New or Different Action

Your power sound bite should discuss actions and ideas you want the audience to consider and adopt. This sounds simple, but it's amazing how many presentations have the audience wondering, "What does he or she want us to do?" Lots of speakers don't consider that a presentation is always meant to influence, as well as inform. Audience members are ready to be introduced to your way of thinking. Remember, they gave you the limited power of conference room dictatorship. Don't ruin all your hard work by presenting a ton of facts without requesting a new action or thought process from audience members.

- Good power sound-bite example: *The only way to ensure success in the years ahead is to take time every six months to study the changes that software developments are making on the accounting industry.*
- Weak power sound-bite example: *Changes in software developments in the accounting industry will have long-reaching effects.*

Critique: The strong power sound bite gives the audience direction. The weak PSB leaves it to the audience to figure out what to do.

Let's go one step further and take a look at three different power sound bites in specific presentation scenarios that could be delivered. Then, we will examine the effectiveness of each PSB and choose a winner.

Power Sound Bite in Action: The Sales Presentation Scenario

You are the lead salesperson for a company that manufacturers printed circuit boards. You're delivering a presentation to the head of engineering and the purchasing manager for a major consumer electronics manufacturer. They know your company has expanded operations and has a good track record for quality, but they have never bought from such a small player in the industry before. Let's take a look at three different power sound bites that you can build your presentation around to convince them to buy from you.

Power sound bite A: *We may not be the largest, but we're the best.*

Power sound bite B: *We offer the most innovative engineering solutions in the industry.*

Power sound bite C: *When you invest in our circuit boards, you're investing in a partner concerned about every single component that comes off your line.*

Let's give each power sound bite an evaluation and examination.

A: WE MAY NOT BE THE LARGEST, BUT WE'RE THE BEST

- Weakness: It's defensive. That's a poor basis of any presentation. Every time you admit a failing or weak market position, you're giving aid and succor to the enemy, the bigger guys, who do not need your help.

- Weakness: It's a cliché. Over-used expressions become meaningless to the audience and cause them to tune out. It is hackneyed and has a facetious ring as if to echo a line out of the *Little Rascals:* "Aw, heck mister, woncha' give us a chance? We ain't the biggest around, but we sure are the best. Let us put on your show." Yeah, whatever.

- Weakness: It's all about you. It's a description, not a call to action for your prospect. "I have a dream" was not about Dr. Martin Luther King Jr. It was a call to action for harmony, peace, and fairness. "We have nothing to fear" was a call for economic optimism and the end to the paralysis of self-doubt. "Are you better off" was a rhetorical chiding of the current administration and a call for a change in leadership.

B: WE OFFER THE MOST INNOVATIVE ENGINEERING SOLUTIONS IN THE INDUSTRY

This is a step in the right direction: stronger than power sound bite A, but not great.

- Strength: It has confidence and power. It also has none of the self-deprecation of the previous example A.

- Strength: It's an intriguing boast, one that could make the potential customer's ears perk up. You are making a grand claim about one of their favorite subject matters, their industry. They might stay tuned to see if you can back it up.

◆ Weakness: It's still all about you, not about the prospect. If you're going to brag about how great you are, it's important to mention how the audience will benefit from your greatness. By not mentioning your audience in the power sound bite, you're missing an opportunity to make a strong connection.

C: WHEN YOU INVEST IN OUR CIRCUIT BOARDS, YOU ARE INVESTING IN A PARTNER CONCERNED ABOUT EVERY NEW COMPONENT THAT COMES OFF YOUR LINE

This is a great example of a power sound bite that rocks!

◆ Strength: It's all about the (audience) prospect: "you invest," "new component," "your line."

◆ Strength: It's specific, direct, and elegant. It says, "What you buy from us will help your company" with charm and aplomb.

◆ Strength: Great action-oriented descriptive words: "investing," "partner."

This winning PSB is a strong example of what can work in almost every sales presentation. By making your power sound bite a positive statement about the relationship you're proposing, you've connected all the dots for the audience. They are now listening.

Creating Your Presentation Around Your Power Sound Bite

If you've got your power sound bite down and you're proud of it, you're ready to build the rest of your presentation. Now, I want you to create the three best statements that support your power sound bite. These should be action-oriented items that you want the audience to consider. Employ the same exercise we used to create the power sound bites.

I want the audience to remember (power sound bite) *and they will understand why we should* (supporting statement #1).

Repeat that exercise two more times.

I want the audience to remember (power sound bite) *and they will understand why we should* (supporting statement #2).

I want the audience to remember (power sound bite) *and they will understand why we should* (supporting statement #3).

Now you're ready to drive home your message of hope and enlightenment. You have created a power sound bite and specific action items that support your main idea. Add some cool stories (see chapter 3), and you'll be ready to be cast in the *Presentation S.O.S.* adaptation of *The Treasure of the Sierra Madre:* "Fears, we don't need no stinking fears!"

Let's take a look at how this plays out with one of the winning power sound bites we've already created.

Power sound bite and supporting statement #1: *You are the best team in the region. You are the ones who will show everyone else how to achieve superior results. I'm delighted and honored to lead you in your efforts. And you will understand why we should change the way we service our customers, ending our county-by-*

county sales-tracking efforts and creating a system that tracks the success of each product in our line. (Discussion of benefits of moving from the county-by-county to the product-mix strategy.)

Power sound bite and supporting statement #2: *You are the best team in the region. You are the ones who will show everyone else how to achieve superior results. I'm delighted and honored to lead you in your efforts. And you will understand why we should all accept and then master the new customer database system that our headquarters has invested in.* (Discussion of new software system and how it will help team.)

Power sound bite and supporting statement #3: *You are the best team in the region. You are the ones who will show everyone else how to achieve superior results. I'm delighted and honored to lead you in your efforts. And you will understand why we should congratulate and support Jennifer, who I am now promoting to regional district supervisor.* (Discussion of Jennifer's new duties and why her strengths are suited for the job.)

The power sound bite sets the stage for three action statement ideas:

1. Changing the sales-tracking system
2. Learning new software
3. Accepting Jennifer as the new district supervisor

All three items are unified under the one power sound bite that says, "This is what we have to do to be the best." When you develop three statements to support your PSB, you've got your presentation laid out. There's no mysterious triangle strength or "power of the pyramid" thesis behind my advocacy of three supporting statements. This manageable number quickly divides the body of your talk into thirds. The audience will find it easy to follow and you will organize your thoughts smoothly. I like it and have seen it work for many good speakers. If you want four supporting statements, go nuts, go crazy, have at it. As long as all of your supporting statements provide great action items for the power sound bite, it doesn't matter how many you use.

When you have your PSB and three supporting ideas, you're on solid ground to deliver a powerful presentation. Get these ideas down on paper/computer screen and you're ready to play ball with the great presenters you've heard and admired. In chapter 5, I'll show you how to use the ever-present PowerPoint to help you get your power sound bite and supporting statements on the screen in front of you, quickly and efficiently, to make them look and sound just the way you want.

Repeat, Repeat, and Then Repeat Again

I agree with those communication mavens who say you need to repeat your key messages over and over. I disagree with their rationale that "the average person needs to hear something six times before it sinks in." I think you have to repeat your key message over and over because *you may not be that good the first time.* When I say *you,* I mean everybody: me, you, even "them." Don't take any chances with your power sound bite. Repeat it often during your presentation.

Great speakers never take it for granted that the audience

will hear everything they say. They know they have to battle to keep the audience members in the room with them, not drifting away. You never know whether you are winning the hearts and minds of the audience members at any given moment. The only way to stay on top is to repeat your power sound bite every few minutes of your presentation. Hitting your PSB again and again gives your presentation a beat and a cadence that creates a very comforting atmosphere for the audience.

Action items for your next presentation:
1. Create a power sound bite that
   - is about the audience.
   - is direct, strong, and simple.
   - is not defensive.
   - asks the audience to take new or different actions.
2. Create three statements that support your power sound bite.
3. Organize your thoughts, ideas, and facts under those three statements.
4. Plan to repeat your power sound bite early and often.

Now get ready to learn how to tell stories.

3

Move Your Presentation from Good to Great: Learn to Tell a Story

WHAT YOU WILL LEARN FROM THIS CHAPTER:

- Why you need to tell stories to support your power sound bite.
- How you can learn to tell stories, right now.
- How stories boost your executive presence.
- Why you should lose all those quotes from famous people.

Storytelling is the ingredient that will take your presentation from good to great, from helpful to inspiring. The power sound bite and supporting statements will make it good, creating a strong connection with the audience. Now I want you to craft and deliver an insightful story to make each supporting statement come alive for the audience. And I'm going to show you exactly how to do it.

Deliberate and well-placed stories give your presentation life and forge an even stronger bond with the audience. Paint a picture with words, helping them see what you see, and you will make your presentation a force to be reckoned with. Stories make facts comforting. Stories make cold figures and seemingly distant concepts reassuring. Stories build connections.

- No five-year-old begs Grandpa for another bedtime "recitation of facts."
- The warm and engaging host or hostess is never "just full of great facts."
- Coffee-room chatter on Monday morning never centers on "wild and crazy facts about the weekend road trip."
- Telephone lines between best friends do not burn with the words: "Have I got a juicy set of facts for you!"

It's the stories that make facts come alive for every audience. I'm convinced nobody wants "just the facts, ma'am," even if they say they do. They want to know what the facts are, as well as what they mean. You need stories to do that. Your audience will rarely be filled with the stern, grim, last-word-getting Joe Fridays. I've observed thousands of audiences, and the specter of Jack Webb hasn't appeared once. Audiences hope to be inspired, guided, and exposed to new ideas and concepts. If they really wanted just the facts, they wouldn't show up to see and hear you. Instead, they'd just ask for an e-mail or a memo.

We all secretly wish to be that speaker who walks through the door and instantly increases the energy level in the room. This is the woman (or man) who connects with the audience right away, commanding attention to her agenda not only with intensity, but also with humor. Her power sound bites always grip the audience, and from the start she has connected the audience to her supporting statement. Perhaps you envy her for her God-given talent, thinking to yourself, "Well, sure, she makes it look easy. She's a natural. Always has been!"

It's okay to be envious, but please shift your focus. You can covet the work ethic, but don't bemoan your personal bad luck in not snaring any "natural communicator" DNA. I believe the "natural" is not a natural: She's working harder at crafting and telling stories than you. This is the shift in mind-set that I want to nudge you toward. Being a great presenter is not a heaven-sent treasure that falls in your lap. It's an acquired trait that I'm going to help you acquire. So go ahead and envy Tiger Woods's low scores, Eddie Van Halen's drum solos, and Meryl Streep's ability to draw you into her character no matter what the accent or time period. I agree that neither you nor I will ever have those talents.

But you can be just as strong as even the best presenters you've seen at the podium. All you have to do is learn how to bolster your power sound bite and supporting statements by developing and then using your storytelling muscle. You don't have to act like other speakers to be strong and successful. You just need to learn how to tell your own stories.

Lots of my clients complain, "I'm just not good at that entire storytelling thing. And I'm never going to be good at it. That's just not my style. I've done pretty well without being sensitive and touchy-feely. I'm not going to change." I say this is a losing attitude. You're giving up a lot when you stick to the macho "I'm not much for spinnin' yarns" protestation. You're giving up things like greater career advancement, better working relationships with your colleagues, a better reputation in your industry, more financial rewards, and greater professional satisfaction. If you still decide to stick to your plan of not investing in storytelling skills, at least know the substantial rewards you're passing up. You're also throwing away a lot of the value you just created in developing your PSB and supporting statements. Become "the total package" and learn to tell stories.

Joe Friday "just the facts, ma'am" stubbornness is a waste. The days of the strong silent type are over, if they ever really existed at all. Ward Cleaver wouldn't command respect at home with June, Wally, and the Beav these days, let alone at the office. Audiences are turned off by presenters who spout clichés supported only by numbers and charts. Audiences want to follow and learn from speakers who are inspiring and who make critical messages come alive with stories and word-pictures.

There's a formula for telling stories and a process for strengthening your verbal picture-painting muscle. It's easy to learn but requires concentration and practice to master. There's good news. Once you've got it, you've got it!

The results are worth it. You'll feel more comfortable at the podium and continue to trounce those gnawing fears from chapter 1. You'll find yourself developing a comfortable internal beat and reassuring consistency as you prepare for every audience and every speaking opportunity. You'll also start to garner a reputation for doing a good job in front of others, and that's a tremendous career asset.

You've got some work ahead of you, but it will be pleasant. Please don't worry that you'll be forced to summon creativity, artistry, sensitivity, or any other trait you've already convinced yourself you don't possess. All you need is a desire to please and connect with the audience. It's a worthwhile investment of your time and effort. Giving the audience a reason to care about your agenda beyond facts and industry jargon makes your professional star rise in everyone's eyes.

Telling stories calls for focus and clarity, just like any great accomplishment—lowering your golf score, delighting dinner guests with a new recipe, or mastering the commands of TiVo.

A protocol exists for transforming a presentation of facts, figures, and jargon into a moving presentation; it inspires your audience to take your side. Moving from fact teller to storyteller involves these steps:

- *Step 1:* Expand your presentation to include a series of details about at least one real or hypothetical person you can name.
- *Step 2:* Replace numbers and industry jargon with the decisions, challenges, and actions of your real person.
- *Step 3:* Describe the result of those actions.
- *Step 4:* Tell the audience why they should care. This becomes a strong signal to the audience about the importance of your power sound bite and supporting statements.

A short, staccato presentation is rarely inspiring or memorable. Well-crafted and well-delivered stories pull the audience toward your power sound bite. Invest more time and energy in creating your stories. The speakers you think "are just naturals" do this. When you learn how to craft stories, you'll be the speaker others are jealous of. You'll have the opportunity to tell your admirers how you aren't a natural, that you've learned to tell stories to make your presentations stronger.

Following are three different presentation scenarios, with two approaches in each. The first is the professional, accurate-yet-bland Joe Friday presentation style; the second demonstrates a contrasting, dynamic, storytelling style. We'll compare them and go over the specific details that make the storytelling style more compelling.

Presentation I: Information Technology Sales Call

Presenter: Salesperson for IT consulting company
Audience: Management team of prospective client
Goal: Describe your company to prospect

The Joe Friday approach: *We're systems integration specialists who can help increase efficiency in your operation. We'll help you leverage your current assets with our sophisticated database of new technology options, promoting greater returns, all the while treating you to a group of individuals who like to consider themselves the "go to team." We see ourselves as the strategic and tactical partners who can take you to the next level. Our world-class professionals are dedicated to taking advantage of a broad array of industry best practices.*

The storytelling approach: *The best way for me to tell you about us is to tell you about Allyson, our senior project manager. Last week she was working with a client on the West Coast who had just gone through an acquisition and was going to scrap the two competing legacy systems and start over from scratch. Here was Allyson's recommendation: "Don't buy any new computers." After a couple days on-site, she realized that with some new custom software, the existing systems could easily work together. The clients would wind up spending $600,000 instead of $3 million. The president of the company couldn't believe his ears. He was so bowled over by the recommendation, he offered Allyson and her family the use of his house in the mountains for a week this summer.*

When you work with us, you get people like Allyson. And we've got many stories just like this one. We know that for your company to make more money every quarter, your computers have to work together to serve your customers and to give you accurate information quickly about how much money you're spending. We're looking forward to the opportunity to work with you.

STYLE COMPARISON

Expansion beyond facts. The bland presentation is 82 words. The storytelling presentation is 196 words. Stories take more words, more sentences, more thought, and more energy. And that's what the audience wants. If your story is meaningful, the audience will be grateful, not impatient. Longer presentations that are filled with rich stories always leave a stronger impression with the audience than short, less-inspired presentations. Cut statistics that add minor benefits if you have to, but make the stories rich and full.

Replace the jargon and numbers with people. In the storytelling presentation, "Allyson" is a real person. You can tell she's smart and dedicated to her clients' success. In the Joe Friday presentation, "system integrators" is an industry label that doesn't leave anyone feeling warm and fuzzy. More like cold, bored, and wondering if the guy talking in jargon just got his MBA last month and is showing off his new vocabulary. Vague promises to "help increase efficiency in your operation by leveraging your current assets" mean little to the prospect and lack conviction.

Even though "systems integrators" is a completely accurate and succinct label, it doesn't help the audience understand you or your power sound bite. Accuracy and brevity do not help you create a connection to the audience. I can't imagine anyone waking up in the morning, stretching, and then proclaiming this technically accurate thought: "Today, I need to leverage my current assets." Real people in real situations don't talk like that. Guys who write brochures talk and write like that because they think it sounds impressive. I think it sounds empty and hollow.

The storytelling presentation is real and full of sincerity. It's a gripping experience for any prospect to hear. Allyson recommends low-cost software instead of expensive new hardware. That's something every buyer would want to experience and would like to consider investing in. I *do* imagine managers, executives, even normal people waking up in the morning, stretching, and saying, "Today, I need to save more money."

Better or worse because of action? The Joe Friday presentation has promised to "promote greater returns." The storytelling presentation offers a concrete example of $2.4 million in savings for the client, when you take the time to do the math (more on eliminating as many numbers as possible in chapter 6). And it doesn't matter what the number is. It could be more or less. The story even works with no number. What counts is that Allyson helps you conserve cash.

Why should we care? The storytelling presentation promises the prospect that you can have someone like Allyson, who knows how to save millions of dollars, on your side. The bland presentation assumes "world-class professionals dedicated to industry best practices" is a real closer. I think it's weak, and if you have a healthy dose of sarcasm in your bones like I do, it's the type of statement that makes you laugh. What are "world-class professionals" anyway? Are they better than "hemisphere-class professionals," or "world-class semi-professionals?" Maybe we could get two of them for the price of one world-class professional.

What do these business school brochure platitudes mean when they come out of your mouth? "Jack Squat!" as the late Chris Farley's inspirational speaker Ned Foley would say. You never have to say "world-class" anything when you can talk about Allyson and her success. Two or three stories like that and your prospects will hire you knowing they've just invested in world-class professionals, without your having to say it. Stories always beat out jargon and labels in support of your PSB and create a great close for you: "We look forward to the opportunity to work together."

Presentation 2: Capital Budget Request for a Soup Kitchen and Shelter

Presenter: Volunteer committee chair
Audience: Volunteer board of directors
Goal: Describe the pressing need for expanded facilities

The bland approach: *We are not fulfilling the mission of our organization. Our service population is growing faster than we can keep up with their needs. Last year in the second quarter we served an average of 168 meals per day. This year in the same quarter we are averaging 322 meals per day. That's an increase of*

92 percent in just one year. The average time a client spent in our serving line used to be twenty-two minutes. This year that time has increased to fifty-six minutes. This is a disaster. We need to expand our facility by 50 percent. According to our facilities manager, the cost will be $400,000. We need to commit to this right now to fulfill our mission.

The storytelling approach: *We are not fulfilling the mission of our organization. I know because I haven't seen Ronald very much in the last month. When he did show up, I asked him where he'd been. He said the last time he had dinner with us he waited over an hour in line. He says it's quicker to hunt through dumpsters when he's hungry than to come here. Sadly, he says, he'd rather be with us. And I'd rather have him here. I know you would too. This is a safe and dignified environment, not an alley. This is a place where at least once a day Ronald will be welcomed and treated with respect.*

But he's worried he may have to wait in line over an hour and that we might run out of food by the time it's his turn. It's a sad moment for all of us when Ronald would rather take his chances in the dumpster than be with us.

Ronald is our client. We are not doing a good job serving him and hundreds of others like him in our current facilities. We need more preparation areas, more ovens and stoves, more serving lines, and more clean and safe places for Ronald to sit. I want to see Ronald having dinner with us, not scrounging in a dumpster. He deserves better than that, as all our clients do. It's going to cost $400,000, and I want to show you why it's a good investment for our facilities and for our community.

STYLE COMPARISON

Expansion beyond facts. The Joe Friday presentation has lots of numbers. They all add up to a reasonable, emotionless conclusion. They also make the audience work pretty hard at doing math, which always triggers the zone-out switch in minds like mine. The storytelling presentation mentions few numbers, saving them for later in the presentation or in a written report. Instead, you focus on Ronald and his circumstances.

Replace the jargon and numbers with people. The bland presentation mentions "service population." I wonder if this bizarre bureaucratic coupling of words could be any chillier to the blood. It may sound accurate in the agency conference room, but at the food line you'll see real men and women showing up for a daily hot meal—people who are a son or a daughter to someone, an uncle and aunt to someone else. The storytelling presentation introduces us to Ronald, a real man, with real human concerns. The bland presentation has many numbers, which calls for the audience to think a lot about math. That has a dulling effect. The action and images in the storytelling presentation are powerful and moving. They portray Ronald's sadness at having to look in dumpsters for dinner. This method is far more memorable and has greater impact than number after number.

Better or worse because of action? In the Joe Friday presentation, the audience realizes that the food line will move faster, but they don't know what that really means. We have to guess that "the service population" will "be processed more quickly."

That's a line worthy of the heartless Old Man Potter from *It's a Wonderful Life*. In the storytelling presentation, the audience envisions Ronald eating his hot meal in a safe, clean environment, instead of on the street.

Why should we care? Both presentations have the same supporting statement backing up a previous power sound bite. Both tell us why we should care. The first presentation hopes the audience will care about improving the numbers. The second outlines what is necessary to bring Ronald back. It's George Bailey at his best, fighting to keep the Bailey Building and Loan alive.

Presentation 3: Safety Meeting at Manufacturing Plant

Presenter: Human resources manager or shift supervisor
Audience: Employees and managers
Goal: Stop the alarming rise in job-related accidents at the plant

The Joe Friday approach: *Safety is our number one concern, but you'd never know it looking at our accident reports. Year to date, our accident incident reports are up 18 percent over last year. Lost work time is up 26 percent. This is simply unacceptable. I see guys not wearing eye protection when they should. I see ladders in our inventory area that are not secured. I see sloppiness all around and an overall lack of attention to the basics of safety. I'm here to tell you it's going to stop right now. I will not tolerate this lackadaisi-*

cal attitude toward safety. From this moment forward, if I see you are not following the safety rules, I'll send you home immediately and dock your pay. I don't care how busy we are. These accident reports are going to get to an acceptable level, or else.

The storytelling approach: *There are signs all over this place reminding you all to work more safely, but they aren't doing any good. Let me tell you why we're having this meeting and why our safety record has to improve. When we don't follow the safety rules we're risking the happiness of the people most important to us. Frank (motions to Frank), I know you coach your son's little league team. It's difficult to hit grounders to the infielders with a broken wrist. Michael (motions toward Michael), I know you and your wife love to fish on the weekends. You can't navigate the lake, manage the depth finder, and hook those walleyes if you're hobbling around with a strained back. When you get hurt, it means I've got to call your loved ones and tell them to meet me at the clinic or the hospital . . . that you're in pain and you need them. I hate making those calls. I hate delivering bad news to your family. And from today on, I'm not going to have to do it. Here's why: If I see any of you not following safety features we've all agreed on, I'm going to send you home instantly. Then you explain to the family why you're not at work. Our safety record will improve starting today because I want you to go home safely tonight and every night.*

STYLE COMPARISON

Let's take a look at why one presentation is strong and why one is average and predictable.

Expansion beyond facts. You might think the Joe Friday presentation is a grand slam because it's tough and the type of tongue-lashing you might have heard in business environments where safety is an issue. I believe speeches like that tend to fall on deaf ears. And for good reason. It doesn't address the audience, the ones who could get hurt. It addresses the corporate track record and gives negative recognition. Once the employees sense the supervisor is more worried about management reports and numbers than broken arms and lacerations, they won't listen. The storytelling version is expansive, yet just as stern. This demonstrates that using stories to back up PSBs does not weaken the presentation. Great presenters aren't afraid of coming up with unpleasant images (your spouse dropping everything to run to your hospital bedside) to drive home their power sound bite.

Replace the jargon and numbers with people. The Joe Friday approach is all about numbers and percentages and track record. The storytelling approach is about Frank the little league coach, Michael the weekend angler, and everyone's spouse. It's easy to see why the storyteller makes a stronger connection.

Better or worse because of action? Joe Friday appears concerned only about himself and eliminating those pesky accident reports. He thinks his team will be more careful if he says safety is his number one concern. This is laughable and meaningless. What company in a factory environment or on a construction site would ever say that safety is "our number seven concern," or "our number thirteen concern"? Safety has nothing to do with places or rating of importance. Safety is about preventing broken bones and strained backs. Every time I hear a speaker use the expression "number one," I envision fans juiced up in the background of ESPN's College Football Game Day, pushing and shoving in front of the camera, hoisting index fingers in the air and shrieking "wooooo!"

Why should we care? The storytelling presentation makes it easy for everyone to care, no matter what their marital or family status. Everyone has someone who would be called if there was an accident. The only motivation Joe Friday gives us is that if we want him off our collective rear ends, then we should worry about going without pay. I think Joe Friday's communication is worthy of Ebenezer Scrooge. The mental picture of you pulling up in the driveway after being sent home and having to admit to your family that the company cares more about your safety than you do is compelling.

The difference between a boring presentation and a compelling one are stories that drive home your power sound bite and supporting statements. The sooner you start inserting them into your presentations, the more your audiences will connect with what you have to say. I'm not telling you to eliminate all your facts, statistics, and jargon; just make sure they come to life with several good, strong, descriptive stories.

Here's a good rule of thumb: Dive into a story about a real person every five to ten minutes during your presentation. This will add texture and brilliance to every supporting statement for your power sound bite. If you have to cut down on some facts to add the stories, go for it. Your audience will thank you.

You shouldn't be uneasy about becoming a storyteller. You can do it, and if you want to connect with your audience, then you have no choice. Those "snore-fest" speakers who present without stories are delivering nothing more than a set of oral facts. They might as well act like a helpless Dilbert and e-mail everyone from the safety of their own cubicle. A great presenter, which you are now on the way to becoming, knows he or she needs stories to convince the audience members they should care about the power sound bite.

Here's an easier way to think about it: Stories are like tickets to the hearts and minds of the audience members. Without stories, the audience won't let you in, and all those fears we talked about in chapter 1 will become a reality. Learning to craft and tell stories that support your PSB is the next step to quelling the sweaty-palms threat of the chapter 1 fears.

Your Stories Can Cure Bad Posture!

I never coach my clients on what some call "executive presence." Instead, I teach them how to tell stories. Describing and sharing a story that is important to you is the quickest way to gain and sustain great presence at the podium, in front of the room, or even sitting at a conference table. If you're telling a story you believe in, your body language, your eye contact, your posture, your use of your hands, and your animation will be perfect for you and for the audience. I won't trot out all the eighth-grade speech class tips and go through chapter and verse of exactly how to stand, project your voice, and make repeated visual contact with the audience. I don't believe these tips are helpful to speakers who want to get better.

You know how to stand. You know how to raise and lower your voice for meaning. You know how to look others straight in the eye. You just can't bring yourself to do it in front of an audience, and you have no idea how those really strong speakers can. After all, it feels weird and kind of creepy to artificially act things out, and it brings up all those icky fears and dreads from chapter 1. Here's what the "good posture, great eye contact" presenters know that you don't: They know when they're in front of the room telling a story about something they really care about, they always automatically have great presence, posture, and poise.

Most business professionals cannot emote on cue. People who can emote on cue are called actors. But even the most passive business professionals can get that fire in their eyes and quickly become engaging by telling a story about a person they believe in. If you're telling a story about someone you see, someone you know, someone you care about, you will exude confidence and project an inspiring executive presence every time, in front of every audience.

Quotes Suck—Get Rid of Them!

Please allow me to rant. I can't figure out the fascination with peppering a speech with quotes from someone famous. I hear it all the time, and I find it never helps the speaker. When you say, "In the words of . . ." in that tweedy professorial and condescending tone, it creates distance from those sitting in front of you. The audience is there to be inspired by you, not the quote your assistant found on the Internet from Churchill, Gloria Steinem, Oprah, Lincoln, Dr. Phil, John Kennedy, Warren Buffett, Ralph Bunch, Dorothy Parker, Descartes, Spinoza, or Jerry Springer (how did he get on that list?). Besides, those people didn't achieve greatness because they were good at quoting other smart guys in speeches. They came up with their own material, specific to their own agenda. I say that "famous people" quotes, like rows of numbers, are meant for the printed page. They're very easy to find, and very easy to put in a presentation. The audience senses that the presenter took the easy way out by spending five minutes on the Internet, instead of really thinking about and trying to explain the issues that are on the table. Quotes from famous guys do nothing more than create an air of self-importance that bogs presentations down and ruins momentum.

If you feel compelled to quote wizened figures, please, just stop. It's much better to share a story or a lesson we can learn from the wizened figures, rather than just quoting them, as if to say, "Look at me. I'm quite literate." Weak presenters fool themselves into thinking they've really hit a home run with the audience when they use quotes from famous people instead of stories about *real* people, famous or not.

Quote Exception

Please disregard the previous sections if you are providing a quote that you have heard with your own ears, and you support it with a story about that person. The people who make for great quotes include Grandma, Grandpa, husband, wife, Mother, Father, sisters or brothers, any teacher, any mentor, any coach (football, basketball, swimming, cheerleading, chess club, it doesn't matter), the guy at the convenience store you see every day, and the woman who cuts your hair. Please, please quote these people and then tell a story about them. Use that story and that person to support your power sound bite and you are starting to rock.

Here's why: We all have a "nana" or "Coach Fairbanks" in our lives. So, please use quotes if they're quotes that come straight from people you know and care about. They will make your next presentation better.

Action items for your next presentation:
1. Create a specific "story person" who will help you define your presentation agenda.
2. Replace numbers and jargon with specific actions and events that center around your story person and your agenda.
3. Explain how your power sound bite items will affect your story person.
4. Demonstrate to the audience why they should care about your story person and the effect of your power sound bite.
5. Repeat Steps 1 through 4 after every supporting statement.
6. Have confidence that your posture and presence will improve every time you talk about your story person.

7. Get rid of "famous person" quotes you found on the Internet.

8. Enjoy it. (But I don't have to tell you this. You will automatically.)

Now that you know how to flex your storytelling muscle, let's figure out how to get you off on the right foot. Your opening can have the audience glued to you or trying to remember if their tee time is at two or three this afternoon. Let's get their minds off golf and keep them on you!

4

Be Great Fast
(You Can't Overcome a Lame Start)

WHAT YOU WILL LEARN FROM THIS CHAPTER:

- Why you need to connect quickly with the audience.
- How to avoid resorting to tired crutches that cause most presenters to fail.
- How to use your power sound bite as a dynamic start.
- How to create a "story person" for your presentation opening.

Bam! You can connect with the audience right away. No warm-up, no getting used to each other. You can create a bond from the moment you step to the microphone, to the front of the room, or as the heads turn your way at the conference table. Show them value, confidence, and strength all in the first two minutes, and you can be assured they'll stay focused on you and not veer off to grinning la-la land. Blast out of the gates with a great open and you'll keep them with you and not headed for the fantasy draft, the menswear department, or the fifth hole tee box of their minds. This chapter will help you keep them in the room from the moment you start speaking.

I want to use the Internet as an analogy. You have to come out of the block interesting and gripping as soon as you start to speak, just as the home page of a Web site has to be interesting and gripping to keep you from clicking off. Here's an example.

There you are at your desk at home, having just gone through a search on Google. There are the ten sites, with ten brief descriptions in front of you. You highlight one that looks perfect for what you need, click on it, and wait for your information to pop up.

A second or two later the site comes up, and are you ever disappointed. Sure the correct site came up, but it is lackluster, all text, white on black, and seems to go on for pages. No graphics, no Flash (Web animation) effects, no cool tabs, not even bullet points or headlines. This is just an academic paper or some type of thesis. It's not fun to explore. It may have some of the information you need, but it's presented with the least flair possible. This is not what a Web site is supposed to be. Web sites are supposed to be cool by their very nature, as well as educational. This is a waste of time. What was the guy thinking who put this together? Nobody in their right mind would want to sift through this.

There at your desk, you will refuse to "give the Web site some time" patiently exploring, clicking through page after page of bland and boring Times New Roman text and hoping it's going to get better. You're not going to give the Web site five or ten minutes to get rolling, you're not going to be sympathetic and think "Maybe this Web site is just having a bad day. I'll just be thoughtful and wait for it to get out of its rut."

Ruthlessly, you're going to click the "back" arrow on your Internet browser, return to your search results page. You have no remorse about leaving the boring site, worrying about hurting the feelings of whoever put it together. It wasn't interesting, it didn't connect with you, and you're not going to waste another second. You're "outta" here, even though you'd probably learn a thing or two by painfully going through all the text. You've moved on to find another site that is both enjoyable and informative.

That's exactly the thought process going on in the minds of those sitting in front of you, waiting to hear your next presentation. They want you to be good! After all, they showed up to hear you speak. But they aren't going to hang around if you're not interesting. If you're not good, right away, they'll mentally click back to the search choice and wind up somewhere else, anywhere, to get away from you. To stop that click, and to keep their minds focused, you have to connect from the moment you open your mouth.

There is a discipline and a strategy (or is it a tactic? Those two are so easy to mix up!) to connecting in the first two minutes, just as there is to creating a power sound bite and developing interesting stories. If you can follow the protocol and the guidelines I'm going to lay out, you'll be in rare company.

Weak opening statements cause the overwhelming majority of speakers to spend much time digging themselves out of a hole. When you begin your next presentation with a direct and confident connection, you'll be better than most of the thousands of speakers I've seen in the past twenty years.

Most speakers do not start with a bang, and instead unintentionally push the audience members away. How does this tragedy occur time after time (*Oh, the humanity!*)?

I fault these lame and slow starts to years of conditioning and hundreds of bad examples we're all exposed to. Sadly, those weak presenters think they're doing the right thing with their trite opening remarks simply because they've seen so many others begin the same way. They're just doing to their audience what has been done to them over the years. But you can change all that the next time you speak.

Let's stop another cycle of audience abuse right now! I'm going to take issue with a myriad of things you've heard other speakers say, maybe as recently as your production meeting this morning, or your industry conference last month. Please promise, no matter what that little voice or tape recording inside your head says, that you will never, ever, begin your presentation by:

- thanking the audience.
- saying, "I'm really glad to be here."
- telling a joke.
- telling the audience what "I've been asked to speak about."
- apologizing (for anything).
- forcing the audience to give you an enthusiastic "good morning," or "good afternoon."

Let's go through each of these so-called tried-and-true introductions so that you can see how damaging they can be to your presentation and your overall reputation. Once we've removed these duds from our presentation arsenal, we'll work on building instant rapport with the audience.

Do Not Thank the Audience

Blasphemy, I know. Everybody thinks this is a great way to begin. Everybody, that is, who hasn't studied great performers in front of happy and fulfilled audiences.

The Broadway cast of *The Producers* do not clasp hands, raise them above their heads, and bow at the beginning of the musical. They do that at the final curtain, after a strong relationship has been built and value has been delivered to the audience. Even as the audience greeted Nathan Lane's appearance onstage in "The King of Broadway," he didn't turn and thank the audience for the applause. He was concentrating on giving the audience their money's worth.

I've seen the Rolling Stones in concert many times. Mick Jagger has never started the show by thanking me (my Bic lighter in the air) and the thousands in attendance for taking the time out of our busy schedules to listen to him. The same is true of any strong performance in front of any audience. Prince, Madonna, Garth, Beyoncé (during and after Destiny's Child)— all perform first and thank later, once there's applause to acknowledge. Speakers should learn from this lesson.

Why didn't Mick (or Keith Richards for that matter) take time to thank me for allowing him to appear before me, the way every single other sales guy, academic, Rotary, or Kiwanis speaker always seems to do? Performers have a keener insight into their relationship with their audience than most speakers do. They understand the whole "this better be good or I'll click off this Web site" mentality the audience has. It probably comes from being booed, or the fear of being booed. Performers know the audience doesn't want thanks; the audience wants to be inspired, uplifted, educated, and energized. They want you to let them know you take them and their investment time seriously. Thanking them does not do that.

Start your presentation with a bang, not a half-hearted thank-you statement. Despite its thin veneer of correct protocol, I say thanking the audience at the beginning does not help you. It just keeps the audience wondering for a few more sentences whether or not you're going to waste their time. This may seem impolite. Please understand that it is not. It may seem too strident. I disagree. Building an instant connection is the thanks the audience truly wants.

Do Not Tell the Audience How Glad You Are to Be with Them

There's a flaw in telling the audience you're delighted, honored, humbled, excited, or whatever, to be with them as soon as you hit the podium.

"I certainly am happy to be here today" has a strong twinge of Eddie ("Gee, that's a lovely dress, Mrs. Cleaver") Haskell to it. Gushing about delight at being at the podium comes off as insincere and pandering. Why should the speaker claim happiness for being in front of the audience at the very beginning? No relationship or rapport has been established. The audience hasn't been attentive or supportive, other than supplying vacantly hollow applause. Don't feign gratuitous honor at their presence in front of you. You can do better than that by showing respect for their time. Be inspiring and motivating first. We'll get to a demonstration of sincere appreciation later.

Starting with a Joke Is Harder Than It Looks

Sure, you'd like to be as funny as Chris Rock. Who wouldn't? You'd love to hear the chortles of joy and guffaws that Ellen DeGeneres hears when she's in front of the audience. We all crave the ability to make people laugh the way Robin Williams,

Elaine Chow, and Dave Chappelle do. Let me be as blunt as Tony's uncle, Junior Soprano, was in responding to the FBI's questions after his arrest on *The Sopranos*. When the G-men demand more information, Junior scoffs, yeah, and he wants a romantic encounter with Angie Dickinson. (Uncle Jun was much more direct.) His sarcasm translates into: *That's not going to happen!* You may think you're a pretty funny guy, why not start with a joke to get the audience on your side? This is a very low percentage gamble and it rarely hits the jackpot.

I've seen speaker after speaker launch into a "funny little story" at the beginning of their presentations. These stories are generally feeble and defeating, sucking any positive air out of the room. As professional actors say, "Dying is easy, comedy is hard." And it's not worth the risk.

Telling a joke or an amusing story is the most difficult way to connect with an audience. I don't know why so many speakers dare to place all their professional weight and integrity over such obviously thin ice. Yet several times a year, each of us experiences the discomfort of impending bad karma that ripples through the room when a speaker begins with, "Being here in front of you today reminds me of the time a priest, a minister, and a rabbi went for a swim at the beach." You and everyone else is afraid the joke will:

- be in bad taste.
- be politically incorrect.
- be stupid.
- make us all uncomfortable.

Many times, the speaker dismally makes all four come true. What a lousy start!

Even when hell freezes over and the joke is actually clever or funny enough to allow the audience to laugh, I'm always more relieved than amused. Telling a joke or a funny story is not worth the sense of impending doom you dump on the audience. Moreover, it takes skill, timing, years of practice, and lots of good luck to tell a joke that works. You wouldn't begin your talk by whistling the melody to *Eine Kleine Nachtmusik* or slapping out the drum solo to "In-A-Gadda-Da-Vida" on the podium to try to warm the audience up a little. Why would you try to perform stand-up comedy? It's harder than Mozart or Iron Butterfly, because there are no die-hard fans out there who will smile and at least give you points for trying. Please shy away from the urge to suck all the energy out of the room by trying to be Jerry Seinfeld. The odds are stacked heavily against you.

"I've Been Asked to Speak About" Is a Killer

This is weak for two reasons. First, it sounds like you'd rather talk about something else, but well, heck, you had to change your plans, because you're a great guy, and after all, "this is what they asked me to talk about." I can't figure out why speakers say this. It's awkward and throws off a premonition of impending failure. "If I could only speak about what I really want to speak about, things would be so much better."

Second, it's delivered in passive voice. This is the part of the book where I get to make my father, the English teacher, really proud. In fact, I'll make every English teacher proud by admonishing you to get rid of all the passive voice delivery in your speech from beginning to end. Don't be embarrassed if you can't put your finger on the difference between active and passive voice. I can't either, but I know the difference when I hear it and see it, so here goes my lesson.

Passive voice ("I was told," "I was asked," "I had been directed") has speakers sounding uncomfortable and wimpy, as if they don't accept responsibility for their own actions. When you use it, you give off vibes that you're insecure and that you have no active voice. A direct tone and active voice ("I'm here today to tell you," "My goal is that you remember," "Barbara mentioned to me") puts the audience on notice. It says their time is valuable and so is yours, so let's dance!

Passive voice has a defeating tone not only at the beginning of your presentation. It is a downer anywhere in your presentation. Be strong, active, and direct in all your statements. Nobody is inspired, informed, or wants to follow someone who is passive. Audiences respond to strength and conviction.

If you seek more depth of knowledge than I can provide about the passive/active voice struggle, Purdue University has a good Web site: http://owl.english.purdue.edu/handouts/grammar/g_actpass.html.

No Apologies!

Unless you unload a cacophonous burp or lose your lunch on the way up to the podium, please don't begin with an apology.

The audience would rather not hear about your shortcomings. Remember, they've given you their time. They're probably not interested in excuses or apologies. They want to be rewarded with your intensity, not your pleadings for forgiveness. They also aren't all that interested in what's wrong. So, if something's not perfect in your world, forget about it. Your perfection is not that important to them. Your enthusiasm, your delivery, your power sound bite, your supporting ideas, and your stories are important. The following examples of worthless apologies always put the speaker at a disadvantage.

- *I'm sorry I have to shorten this presentation for you. Normally I get more time.*

What an ego from the speaker who says this! Believe me, nobody in the audience is shouting "Drat!" at the lack of time to demonstrate your brilliance. Let them judge whether or not your talk is good enough to warrant their time. Ten, fifteen, or forty-five minutes: Whatever your slot is, just be great. Don't let them know you are frustrated at the lack of time.

- *I'm sorry this isn't the most current version of my PowerPoint presentation. It's a version from last quarter.*

I can put your mind at ease on this one. Tears are not welling up in the corners of every eye in the room. The audience members are not getting a lump in their throat, churning inside because you are missing a few slides. They won't know. They won't care. Keep the transgression to yourself. Somehow, some-way, the audience will survive to see another day.

◆ *I'm sorry I'm here instead of the speaker/program you were supposed to have.*

This is a pitiful way to begin a presentation. It sounds like the speaker is pleading for a compliment, or is extremely inse-cure about his or her abilities. The best way to make it up to them is for you to be great. Get to your power sound bite fast. Follow it with a compelling story. The audience will forget all about what's his name and be glad that you're in front of them.

Apologies are usually unnecessary and can put the audience in tremendous discomfort. Give them something positive at the beginning of your talk, not something negative. You should, however, always apologize for a burp.

Shouting "Good Morning" Is Trouble

This technique to "really get the audience going" was solicitous when it first reared its ugly head in the 1960s (I'm guessing on the date because presentation historians do not have carbon dat-ing at their disposal), and it's worse now. Let me go over the sce-nario with you in case you've been able, unlike me, to erase this unpleasantness from your memory.

The speaker confidently walks up to the stage, adjusts the microphone, and belts out "Good morning," or "Good afternoon." We don't expect the speaker to be toying with us, so we give a mild repartee to the salutation, a gentle nod or a mumbled return, "Good morning."

This speaker is going to whip us into shape, pronto. That's when the speaker steps closer to the microphone and lets us in on the full extent of our disappointing ways by bellowing in full admonishment, "I said, 'Good morning' (or 'Good afternoon')!"

Now, according to ancient and ridiculous tradition, we're all supposed to look sheepishly at each other and quickly pipe up a resounding "Good morning!" Wow, this speaker really means business! After all, we want to curry the speaker's favor, don't we? Then the speaker smiles that self-righteous smile, nods as if he or she has sent us to bed without supper for our own good, and says, "Well, that's better. Now we can get going."

This technique deserves a whole wing in the Lame Presentation Hall of Fame. I find myself torn every time I hear that second, admonishing, "Good morning." I feel pity for myself and the speaker, knowing this is probably not going to be a good experience. At the same time I want to jump up and scream, "My hearing is fine. You just said that. And oh yeah, just because you yell, 'Good morning' at me, does not mean I will be shamed into shouting it back at you. I heard you the first time, ya' moron. You're here to help and inform me, not make me grovel before you. Now, buddy, let's get going with whatever you're going to tell us. Time is money!"

The "good morning" repetition never warms up the audience. It makes them want to cover their ears and hide their eyes.

There's Nothing Left to Say!

I've just put the international "no" sign on every technique that's been foisted upon you since you've been a member of an audience. No thanking, no "really glad to be here," no jokes, no telling what you've been asked to speak about. No apologizing. No patronizing "good morning" commands. What the heck is left, you say?

How about just being great from the moment you open your mouth? You can do it and the audience will be glad. Following are two different "power open" techniques that you can use, starting now. One calls for discipline and protocol, the other calls for imagination and creativity. Depending on your audience and your mood, pick one you want to use for your next presentation. They're both easy to master.

Power Open #1: Your Power Sound Bite Is Your First Sentence

Some of you may feel this technique is too pushy. Shouldn't we get comfortable with each other before we get right to the agenda? You don't want to be too forward, do you? That's bound to put people off. If that's what you think, you're confusing the protocol of a romantic courtship with the protocol of a presentation.

Here's my advice: Take your time on a date, but cut straight to the intimacy in your presentation. That first date is just the start of the relationship that may blossom over months and years. The presentation *is* the relationship. It will be over in thirty to forty-five minutes. They may never see you again, but you still have to connect with them. You have to establish instant intimacy. Everything has to move at warp speed.

Remember the fears of chapter 1. The audience will not give you the time or the patience to get to know you. They want excitement, wit, intellect, and fulfillment. And they want it right now. They aren't looking for you "to complete them." They get that from someone else in their lives. They're looking to make this thirty to forty-five minutes worth their while. Going slow is not a good idea. Getting right to your power sound bite tells the audience, "This is going to be good, so listen up."

Here are some scenarios that prove the PSB open works. One follows the "go slow/dating" protocol. The other follows the "one shot fling" power sound bite protocol. You be the judge as to which works better.

Presenter: An analyst in the human resources department of a large financial services company

Audience: The executive committee of an expanding division of the company

Goal: To go over projections for necessary employment level for the next four quarters

GO SLOW OPEN: LACKLUSTER "C" PERFORMANCE

Well, I am certainly glad to be here today to speak to all of you. When Brad asked me to put these numbers together and deliver this presentation, I jumped at the chance because everyone in the

company knows your team is involved in a lot of exciting new proj-
ects. Of course, nothing here is cast in stone, and I'll want to get
feedback from each and every one of you before I deliver my report
to the board of directors. Oh, and by the way, I'll dress up these
PowerPoint slides before I deliver them to the CFO and the board.
I just wanted to get the basic info down for you guys so I could get
some input. Having said that, let me share with you some of the
indicators I studied before coming up with some of my conclusions.
That way, you'll know where I'm coming from, okay?

This is typical of opening remarks we hear all the time. They
aren't offensive, and to the casual listening ear there's nothing
seriously wrong with them. It's just more of the same presentation gruel that's been forced down our throats since the advent
of the conference room. It's nourishing at a subsistence level,
but gruel nonetheless. I'm going to show you how we can do
much better and substitute steak and sizzle for the gruel. First,
let's see why most audiences wouldn't grade this presentation
open any better than a "C."

I broke many of my presentation open rules to show how
they play out in the typical slow open. Let's go through this
open, sentence by sentence, evaluating it with the sarcastic and
judgmental ear of the audience member who's been burned by
too many lousy presentations in the last month.

◆ *Well, I am certainly glad to be here today to speak to
all of you.* (—Goody. I'm glad you're glad. Now I
can lead a full life.)

◆ *When Brad asked me to put these numbers together for you and deliver this presentation, I jumped at the chance because everyone in the company knows your team is involved in a lot of exciting new projects.* (—Are you trying to polish Brad's apple, or are you blowing smoke on all of us? Stop being so patronizing.)

◆ *Of course, nothing here is cast in stone, and I'll want to get feedback from each and every one of you before I deliver my report to the board of directors.* (—Thanks for the chance to do more work that will help you. And while you're at it, dump the "cast in stone" garbage. We know you need our blessing to move forward with this.)

◆ *Oh, and by the way, I'll dress up these PowerPoint slides before I deliver them to the CFO and the board. I just want to get the basic info down for you guys so I could get some input.* (—You have us confused with someone who cares about the artistic quality of your PowerPoint. And since you're using the expression, "oh, and by the way," let us do the same and say, "oh, and by the way," thanks for telling us this is just a scratch copy and you'll make it better for the guys who are really important to your career.)

♦ *Having said that, let me share with you some of the indicators I studied before coming up with some of my conclusions. That way, you'll know where I'm coming from, okay?* (—Great, I'm on the edge of my freaking chair, wondering about the brilliant process of your research and deductive powers, okay? Get to the point, okay? How many people are we going to have to recruit, hire, and train? Let's go, okay?)

Ouch! Audiences aren't typically that mean, but they can be if the speaker is wasting their time. This is not a bad thing and the best speakers know that. You can win the audience over by moving faster, dumping patronizing yet seemingly polite expressions, and getting on with making the best use of everyone's time.

POWER SOUND BITE OPEN: "A" PERFORMANCE

I'm here to tell you that you're going to have a challenging assignment in the next fiscal year, because you're going to be doubling your number of employees. You're going to see twice as many faces at your division meetings, you're going to have to rent and build space for twice as many workstations, and unless these new guys aren't caffeine addicts like the rest of us, you're going to have to buy twice as much coffee and soda to keep them going every month. Lots of work ahead, but I say you're lucky! Everybody else I talk to across the country wishes they could have such growing pains. Now, these are my predictions for you that I'm going to pass along to the board, as soon as I get your approval. Let me show you how I came up with my numbers, so you can make sure I'm on the right track.

This is a great open. Let's examine why, sentence by sentence.

◆ *I'm here to tell you that you're going to have a challenging assignment in the next fiscal year, because you're going to be doubling your number of employees.*

The first sentence answers the audience's questions and takes their feelings into account, understanding this is going to be a ton of work for them.

◆ *You're going to see twice as many faces . . .*

This portion of the open incorporates the storytelling techniques of chapter 3. The speaker isn't just talking about the new payroll positions, but the work it takes to hire and house twice as many employees. This portion also uses slight situational humor (as opposed to a heavy-handed joke) painting a picture of hardworking coffee addicts in the break room. It describes a vibrant, growing environment in a very time-efficient manner.

◆ *You're lucky! Everybody else I talk to across the country wishes they could have such growing pains.*

This is a pleasant, non-patronizing compliment.

◆ *Now, these are my predictions for you that I'm going to pass along to the board, as soon as I get your approval. Let me show you how I came up with my numbers, so you can make sure I'm on the right track.*

This is polite, appreciative, and thoughtful. It creates a respectful environment in the room that should have the audience listening and adding input. This all adds up to a winning open.

Power Open #2: Make Your Open About a "Story Person"

I hope I've convinced you not to use the boring, slow open. Also, we've looked at the benefits of using your power sound bite as your opening sentence that will drive the introduction of your presentation.

Now, let's go for the golden ring. Here's an open technique that's even stronger than the PSB open. It takes more thought, more time, and more storytelling muscle. It's also the fastest way to grab the audience by the lapels. Or as the surfer dude from chapter 1 says, "Let's party!"

Consider delaying your power sound bite until the last sentence of your open. Instead, try talking about one person, imaginary or real, who best demonstrates the results, actions, and consequences of your power sound bite. Let's see one example that demonstrates how powerful it is. We'll work off the same scenarios, the human resources statistician providing a labor projection to a fast-growing division.

◆ *I'd like to talk about a woman you don't know. Her name is Yolanda, and she works at Financeco* [a fictional competitor]. *She's sharp, has a great way with clients, has a decade of experience under her belt, and definitely is an asset for our competitor. But, alas, Yolanda is grumpy. She wants more opportunity and wants to work for a winner. She's not the type to jump ship quickly, but she wants to realize her ambitions. To do that she wants to work with a dynamic company, not a stale one. I'm telling you about Yolanda today, because you're going to be seeing a lot of her in this conference room, at the coffee machine, the elevators, and your monthly softball games. That's because you're going to have to hire Yolanda in the next twelve months. And she's not the only one. Just to keep up with your workload, you're going to have to double your head count in the next fiscal year. That's a lot of industry stars like Yolanda to find, recruit, and get in place and to train. It's going to be hard work, but it's a job the guys in the other divisions tell me they'd love to be facing. Let me show you the process I went through to come up with the "Operation Yolanda" initiative. I want to make sure I've done my homework correctly for you.*

It's easy to pay attention to this story, because it's about a real person, whom all of us would like to have in the next office. It's telling the audience members, "You'll have more work ahead of you, but it is the work that comes from success." It paints a picture as a lead-in to the power sound bite:

◆ *Just to keep up with your workload . . .*

This makes the power sound bite even more vibrant because it creates anticipation and acceptance for the PSB.

◆ *Let me show you the process I went through to come up with the "Operation Yolanda" initiative. I want to make sure I've done my homework correctly for you.*

This is a great way to ask for help and eventual approval, all the while being respectful of the audience members and their valuable time. Naming the hiring push after the competitor's current employee is a creative way to give credence throughout your presentation to your opening comments.

Telling a story about a person (real or imagined) that you can see and help the audience to see sets the table for your power sound bite. This technique takes more work on your part, maybe ten to fifteen minutes to identify and fill in the characteristics of your story person. Make the investment. Other than ten to fifteen minutes of your time, there's little to lose and a lot to gain. It would be great to have your peers saying five minutes into your presentation, "Wow, what did Ken eat this morning? This presentation is really good. I'm impressed."

Action items for your next presentation:

   1. Banish the presentation opening *don'ts*.

- Do not thank the audience.
- Do not tell the audience how glad you are to be with them.
- Do not start with a joke.
- Do not start with the words "I've been asked to speak about."
- Do not apologize.
- Do not force the audience to give you an enthusiastic "good morning" or "good afternoon."

   2. Develop your power open.

- *Power open #1:* Use your power sound bite as the first words that come out of your mouth.
- *Power open #2:* Create a story around a real or imagined person that creates a strong visual lead-in to your power sound bite.

Now that you've got the open down, let's make PowerPoint your dear friend, instead of a necessary evil.

5

PowerPoint Doesn't Bore Audiences, Lousy Speakers Do (All We Are Saying Is Give PowerPoint a Chance)

WHAT YOU WILL LEARN FROM THIS CHAPTER:

◆ PowerPoint is a strong tool to help you organize, plan, and create order for your next presentation.

◆ PowerPoint can help you bond with your audience during your presentation.

◆ Most presenters misuse PowerPoint, making audiences grumpy.

◆ How to use PowerPoint to make your audience happy, not grumpy.

PowerPoint can be your friend and this chapter will show you how to use it (from a nontechnical perspective) to make your bond with the audience even stronger. PowerPoint can be a delightful frosting and build your confidence. This can all be at your fingertips when you learn to use PowerPoint to your advantage. By following a few simple rules, you can develop a set of PowerPoint slides that will help your presentation soar. What a refreshing change from most of the PowerPoint slides we've been forced to sit through!

What I'm Taking for Granted You Already Know

PowerPoint comes with most computers and allows you to make slides to project to the audience while you are speaking. (You need a projector that allows your computer to do this.) PowerPoint has replaced what our forbearers called "over-heads" the way LCD (liquid crystal display) projectors replaced overhead projectors. I'm going to proceed as if you can already use PowerPoint. If that's not the case, find a computer and spend ninety minutes working the tutorial. That's all the prep you'll need to utilize the program for organizing your presentation and creating slides that will help you connect with your audience.

Personal Disclaimer

I'm not Microsoft certified in PowerPoint. I'm not a computer guy and I've never taken a PowerPoint class. I'm not sure, but I guess I use just a fraction of what PowerPoint has to offer. I use the pull-down menus and if I can't figure out what I want to do, I go to the Help index and spend a few keystrokes trying to figure it out. Usually I just muddle through, and am always happy with my results. I'm just like you! The lesson is not meant to teach you how to use everything PowerPoint has to offer. I don't know everything it has to offer, or how to use it. But I do know how, if you have a minimal knowledge like me, you can use PowerPoint to help make your next presentation great.

PowerPoint: Cooler Than Little Blue Note Cards with Tiny Lines

PowerPoint is a fast, easy, flexible tool that will help you organize, plan, create, and, overall, figure out the direction of your upcoming presentation. As they said on those '70s TV commercials touting Ginzu knives, bamboo steamers, and the Pocket Fisherman, "now what would you pay?" That's right, PowerPoint is a great deal: a powerful, easy-to-use computer tool to get you organized as you plan your presentation. Not only that, it can help you connect with your audience come showtime.

If you don't have anything down on computer screen or

paper yet, you can use PowerPoint right now to get a jump start. Together, you and I are going to create the outline for your presentation. This is the template you can use to organize your thoughts for any presentation. So go ahead, open PowerPoint. You're staring at the first slide of your next presentation.

Slide 1: Type in: *My Presentation Action Title.*
    Click the "new slide" button.
Slide 2: Type in: *My Power Sound Bite.*
    Click the "new slide" button.
Slide 3: Type in: *Supporting Statement #1.*
    Click the "new slide" button.
Slide 4: Type in: *Supporting Statement #1: Data/Info Slide.*
    Click the "new slide" button.
Slide 5: Type in: *Supporting Statement #1: Data/Info Slide.*
    Click the "new slide" button.
Slide 6: Type in: *Supporting Statement #1: Story Slide.*
    Click the "new slide" button.
Slide 7: Type in: *Supporting Statement #2.*
    Click the "new slide" button.
Slide 8: Type in: *Supporting Statement #2: Data/Info Slide.*
    Click the "new slide" button.
Slide 9: Type in: *Supporting Statement #2: Data/Info Slide.*
    Click the "new slide" button.
Slide 10: Type in: *Supporting Statement #2: Story Slide.*
    Click the "new slide" button.
Slide 11: Type in: *Supporting Statement #3.*
    Click the "new slide" button.

Slide 12: Type in: *Supporting Statement #3: Data/Info Slide.*
    Click the "new slide" button.

Slide 13: Type in: *Supporting Statement #3: Data/Info Slide.*
    Click the "new slide" button.

Slide 14: Type in: *Supporting Statement #3: Story Slide.*
    Click the "new slide" button.

Slide 15: Type in: *My Power Sound Bite: Reprise.*
    Click the "new slide" button.

Slide 16: Type in: *My Presentation Action Title.*
    Click the "new slide" button.

If I were twenty-five years younger, I'd say, "Dude, you got yourself a presentation!" Since that's not the case, I'm still happy to say with these sixteen slides you now have a multipurpose outline and template that's a tidy place to organize your thoughts and ideas. Keep this template close by. It can take the "oh my God, what am I going to do?" fear out of your next presentation.

If you type out these sixteen generic slides, here's what the template for your next presentation, and for all your future presentations, will look like.

- ◆ Introduction: Slides 1–2
- ◆ Body of the talk: Slides 3–14
- ◆ Big close: Slides 15–16

This template will guide you through the process of creating your presentation. It's a road map, game plan, musical score, recipe (enough metaphors for you?) to success in organizing your presentation. If you follow this structure, and the following tips, you'll be able to create a presentation from open to close in a logical order you and the audience can follow. Your sixteen template slides provide a structure that will help you

- develop a strong title.
- develop your power sound bite.
- add the first statement that supports your power sound bite, followed by two data/info slides and a story slide.
- add the second statement that supports your power sound bite, followed by two data/info slides and a story slide.
- add the third statement that supports your power sound bite, followed by two data/info slides and a story slide.
- end with a big close.

Now improvise. Have fun. Add an additional data/info slide for each supporting statement. Throw in one or two more supporting statements with more data/info and story slides, if that's what you need to back up your PSB. There's no rule of thumb for the total number of slides you should wind up with. If you begin with this template you'll have a good vehicle to create order and eliminate the chaos rumbling around in the head of every speaker (including me) a week or two ahead of a presentation.

This template can also point out where you need to shore up

your presentation. After looking at your sixteen slides you may find some holes where you need to do some homework. If you can't fill all the sixteen slides, especially the data/info and story slides, make some more phone calls, read or do research to help your audience understand your power sound bite.

Word for Word vs. Notes

There are two schools of thought about what you should bring up to the front of the room to help deliver a presentation: bullet points on note cards, or all of the pages of your presentation, printed out word for word. Let me weigh in on what's best: It doesn't matter and it doesn't affect success. I've seen speakers with written speeches knock it out of the park and I've seen them fail, chasing the minds of each audience member to a different astral plane. I've seen men and women with notes rock; I've seen them crash and burn. I like bullet points personally, but I don't necessarily recommend that as the best path to follow. Do whatever is most comfortable for you.

The note versus full-text debate is meaningless when compared to two preparation processes that truly affect your performance. First, you need the correct editorial or "meaty" ingredients we've been working on so hard: power sound bite, supporting statements, and stories. Second, you have to practice. Skip the practice and you're blowing all your hard work. We'll hit practice (how to do it, how many times, etc.) hard in chapter 9.

If you decide to go the notes route, PowerPoint has a good feature for you. You can create a detailed "notes" text slide that tells you what you want to say for every projected slide in your template. Go to the "View" pull-down menu and click on "Notes." Work with it for a while and see if it fits your needs.

Why the Bad Rap on PowerPoint?

PowerPoint is a great organizational tool, even if you never project it on the screen. But if you're going to go ahead and show your slides, there are some rules you need to follow. Let me borrow some syntax from another debate and proclaim, "PowerPoint doesn't bore audiences; lousy presenters misusing PowerPoint bore audiences."

Here's a scene you'll never see: A busy and successful engineer takes a sip of coffee, folds the morning paper in half, turns to the significant other at the kitchen table, and says, "You know what would make this day great? If I could just sit through a forty-five-minute presentation that has a lot of PowerPoint slides! I mean, I'd really love to see slide after slide, just chock-full of numbers and charts and graphs and stuff. I find so many days recently unfulfilling, and I know this would just put a bounce in my step. Yes, sir, a PowerPoint presentation could just turn my lackluster week around. I wonder if this will be my lucky day." You'll never witness this scene, because it's never happened and it never will.

PowerPoint does not create an adrenaline rush for any member of the audience. It does not get an audience "ready to rumble," or send murmurs of suspense and excitement rippling through the crowd. More likely, firing up that projector, leveling the image, and tapping computer keys until the PowerPoint logo flashes on the screen has the same effect as administering a mild barbiturate to the audience. We've been conditioned by hundreds of presentations to expect way too much perplexing data and way too much text, causing eyestrain and headaches. We're sadly conditioned to think that every time PowerPoint hits the screen, we're going to have some real work to do. PowerPoint has been abused so much and so regularly that some managers go so far as to banish it from their meetings.

That's like throwing your stereo out the window because your girlfriend had the audacity to take off your Miles Davis *Birth of the Cool* album and replace it with Barry Manilow's greatest hits. Detest "Mandy" all you want, but don't take it out on the Marantz direct drive turntable! It's the same with PowerPoint. (Barry Manilow fans: Please reverse previous analogy, substitute AC/DCs *Back in Black* for *Birth of the Cool,* and "You Shook Me All Night Long" for "Mandy," and it will all become clear.)

PowerPoint Success: The Rules

Inherently, PowerPoint is a very good tool that, unfortunately, can and will drive audiences to distraction—or worse, forty winks—when placed in the hands of well-intentioned presenters who don't know what they're doing. On the following pages are the best of the rules of PowerPoint conduct.

RULE #1: USE POWERPOINT TO HELP, NOT CONFUSE YOUR AUDIENCE

Video has to match audio. What the audience sees must match what the audience hears. That's the first thing professors teach every television news cub reporter in journalism school. This means get the words down first and then match the pictures to them. This dictum has guided the editing of every television news story you've ever seen: audio first, then video. Television journalists write the words, record them, and then fit the visuals to match. Otherwise, stories would be hard to follow and impossible to edit. It's a critical rule for you to follow as you make your slides.

Each slide should reinforce the audio, in this case, the words coming out of your mouth. That means the information on the screen mirrors and supports your words. Make this a rule for every single slide.

Even experienced speakers struggle with this concept. In the past, executives have tried to explain to me that if the audience can read additional facts on the slides while they're listening to what the presenter is saying, then everyone is better off. They're saying if audience members can read and digest, while listening and digesting, they're getting two for one! I say it's really zero for two! Everybody loses when the words and diagrams on the screen don't mirror what the speaker is saying. Slides that add new ancillary information, instead of simply and easily reinforcing what the speaker is verbalizing, give the audience a headache. The presentation quickly becomes too much work for everyone in the audience and "uh-oh," here comes the fantasy league. Make sure the words, tables, and charts on the screen back up and reinforce the words coming out of your mouth.

RULE #2: TEXT—INTERESTING WORDS, FEWER WORDS, LARGE TEXT

Your slides should give the audience a gentle visual push toward your ideas. Please make certain your slides don't push them away from you. The easier the words are for the audience to read, the better slides flow with your voice. Keep the text large, and limit the number of words on each page. I've seen all kinds of guidelines: ten words per slide, seven words per slide, minimum 22-pica, 26-pica, and so on. I don't have any strict numbers to guide you. Rather, just make sure the words on the screen create seamless reinforcements to the words coming out of your mouth. They don't have to be the exact words, just a few of the helpful, strong words you are speaking.

You can do that by throwing in some dynamic verbs, adjectives, and adverbs—the same way you do when you speak. Add a second line, or subtitle, to add some spice. Make your text fun, powerful, serious, and insightful . . . all in the same presentation. Most of all, don't make it boring. An active, thoughtful title page is a good way to get off to a great start as you plan your upcoming presentation.

Here's an example: Let's imagine you are doing a presentation about last month's continuing low sales.

◆ Ineffective and boring title page:

OCTOBER SALES FIGURES

This title won't send anyone's heart racing or create intense anticipation. It's nothing more than a label, something you'd put on a file folder tab. Slides like this are common, but never inspiring, and don't promote a connection with the audience. This keeps the audience abreast of the current topic coming from the speaker's mouth, but it does nothing else. It shows the speaker didn't prepare much or expend any creative energy to help the audience understand the upcoming presentation. That's not helpful for the speaker, unless his or her goal is to promote lethargy in the room.

◆ Average title page:

OCTOBER SALES FIGURES—OFF THE MARK

Average titles like this don't hurt and don't help the speaker. This does give the audience an idea of what they're going to be hearing about, and hints there might be some interest ahead. However, there is no energy, no punch, and no reason to care or to stay tuned. The speaker can do much better than this with just slightly more effort.

◆ Strong title page:

OCTOBER SALES DISAPPOINTMENT—
WHY WE MISSED THE GOAL

This works on several levels. Strong titles tell the audience what they're going to hear and give them a reason to care. This title adds some emotion ("disappointment") and intellect, telling the audience members that this speaker has gone to real effort to make presentation time in the conference room valuable for everyone.

Remember to keep the word count low, the size of the letter large. This may be the single most helpful tip in this whole chapter and perhaps all of *Presentation S.O.S.* You can help the audience understand your power sound bites and supporting statements easily and quickly if you keep your word count for each slide to the lowest number you feel comfortable with. Make an effort to hone the text on every slide before the presentation. The key to making PowerPoint your ally is to be sure the slides propel the audiences forward and bolster your presentation. Use fewer words, and choose words that are interesting and filled with energy and insight.

RULE #3: GRAPHS AND TABLES—THE SIMPLER THE BETTER

The charts-and-graphs function of PowerPoint is strong and fun to work with. I've seen many speakers fall in love with the ten zillion ways they can import a few highlighted numbers from their Excel spreadsheets and create bar, pie, line, and 3-D charts and graphics—all with a couple of clicks. Speakers frequently display these graphs to the audience with the same sense of pride and accomplishment second graders use when displaying a school art project for their parent: "Look at what I did, Mommy!"

Let me break some sad news to speakers who are enraptured by the charts and graphs they've created: Nobody in the audience will ever admit they are impressed with your bar chart skills. Instead, they'll be impressed with the ability of the speaker to help them simply and easily understand trends, patterns, and issues. The skills are different. Making really cool, detailed, and colorful graphs is no guarantee of success. Creating easy-to-follow charts that back up a compelling PSB is the road to follow for a successful presentation.

This is where many speakers ruin their talks. They think the brilliance, and many times painstaking detail, of the charts helps move their presentation beyond the power of their own words. If that's the case, they should just e-mail the bar graphs to the audience members so they can study the brilliance at their own pace.

If you're going to use charts and graphs in your presentation, here are some specific tips to make sure the slides strengthen your connection to the audience.

Less is more. Keep every slide with a chart or graph simple and uncluttered. You should be able to tell the audience what the slide means in one easy-to-understand sentence. Then go forward and describe how each element of the slide backs up that simple premise. Here's a strong description for a slide about those lousy sales figures:

This slide breaks down our losses for October by product line, and it paints an ugly picture. The blue bar shows how we missed the mark in hardware, the yellow bar shows how we fell behind in service, and the green bar shows we were behind in installation as well.

This is simple and easy to understand. Add the real numbers to the bars if you want to, but make them big and easy to digest. Here's an easy guideline: If you can't explain why the audience should care about the slide in one sentence, then it's not the right slide. Make it simpler.

Similarly, if you can't use one sentence to describe each element of the graph or chart, you've got too much stuff up there. Break your graphs and charts into several more slides that you can easily apply the one-sentence-description rule to.

One final chart and graph note: When you import cells from Excel to PowerPoint, you always get a "legend" in the bargain. The legend is the box that explains what each color on the graph stands for. PowerPoint creates this automatically for your slide. That's a great extra for someone who is going over your chart at the quiet of the desk. Unfortunately, it can be distracting to the audience. Audience members shouldn't have to spend time and energy deciphering that little box to the side of your three bars on the chart while you're speaking. Here's the solution: Delete the "legend" for your presentation. You don't want the audience trying to figure out on their own what the blue bar means and what the yellow area means. It's your job to do that for them.

RULE #4: I NEVER MET A PIECE OF CLIP ART I LIKED

Back in the dawn of computer literacy, let's say 1989, the ability to place a clever little cartoon or artist's rendition in a presentation was a source of complete wonder and amazement. I believe time has passed clip art by. I have not seen a presentation during the past five years that's been enhanced by a slide containing clip art. This despite the fact that PowerPoint, along with the Web, gives you a never-ending cavalcade of cartoons and sketches to choose from.

I don't think highly of clip art because it doesn't create a connection with the audience. No one says, "Oh, isn't that just too funny. That cartoon character is so mad at his computer, he's smashing it with a hammer. Now I understand what the speaker is saying about eliminating stress in the workplace. What a helpful slide!" Clip art, even non-cartoon clip art, does not help the speaker connect with the audience. It looks tired and takes the energy and meaning away from the speaker's words. Here's a good example. Better you show the audience the words "cash flow" on the screen than a big green, 3-D sparkling "$." We see too many fantastic and wonderful images every day on TV and on the Internet that have been custom created by the best computer artists on the planet. Please do not try to compete with them. If you can leave the clip art alone, you'll be able to concentrate on more helpful text and powerful charts.

RULE #5: PICTURES—LOVE THE REAL, DUMP THE STAGED

If you're talking about increased productivity and you've got a pleasant, but not necessarily perfect, photo of your colleagues Jennifer, Bob, Amanda, and Jerome poring over engineering drawings in your conference room, by all means, put it in your presentation! If you've pulled a picture from the Internet with perfect people (perfect smiles, waistlines, and clothes) under perfect lighting and a gorgeous conference room, resist the urge to cut and paste.

When it comes to pictures, the audience reacts positively to real people, real buildings, and real environments. The perfect people in the generic perfect pictures take away from your presentation because this image creates a mild scoff in the minds of the audience. I've worked in thousands of conference rooms over the past twenty years, and I've never seen one with such perfect, happy people and such perfect art direction. If you're going to go for beauty or perfection, you might as well find a rights-free (you don't have to pay the person who owns the rights to a picture) waterfall or calming meadow. My picture rule of thumb: If it can create a positive and real connection with the audience, it is a great tool for you. If more than one person in the picture has perfect teeth, coiffed hair, or the looks of someone who successfully limits fat intake to less than twenty-two grams a day, then it's probably not a picture for you. "We" don't look like those perfect picture guys. There's no reason to feature "them" in our presentations.

RULE #6: BACKGROUNDS—LIKE GRAPHS, THE SIMPLER THE BETTER

PowerPoint comes with a ton of backgrounds, which will automatically give a uniform look and color scheme to your slides. Some of them are simple and some are more detailed. It's interesting and easy to try them out, so have a blast seeing your presentation with different types of art-directed themes. One of them may be perfect for your theme and your anticipated connection with the audience. If you decide to use a background, keep it simple and make sure it maximizes the value of the words on the screen, which should also match the words coming from your mouth.

So go ahead, spend a few minutes playing with the backgrounds. You may find one that perfectly fits the tone and messages of your presentation.

RULE #7: ANIMATION EFFECTS—I LIKE 'EM (SURPRISE!) IN MODERATION

Under the "Slide Show" menu button, there's a tab for animation effects. These allow you (with some additional keystrokes) to animate every element of your presentation: every word, every title, and every graph. Spend thirty minutes or so trying it out and you'll be ready to use this feature in your next presentation.

I like to use animation schemes in a simple and consistent manner. That means "flying" text in from right to left, a full sentence at a time, every time. I like the fact that this animation builds a rhythm, a beat, and a cadence to your presentation that can build more energy in the room. Swoops, whirligigs, and shudder effects don't do the same thing simply because they draw too much attention to themselves.

Explore the animation menu and see whether animation suits you. If not, that is just fine. You can be an outstanding PowerPoint presenter without using a single animation. It's just like adding sprinkles, which you should consider adding to the frosting of your next PowerPoint.

PowerPoint's Biggest Benefit

All these pages and paragraphs on PowerPoint and I haven't even told you my favorite benefit. Every time you change slides, or bring on a new graph, or animate new text on the screen, you have a new opportunity to re-connect with the audience. It can be a subtle, friendly nudge that pleasantly says, "Hey, this is the next thing you need to know." That's why keeping the slides simple, fun, and easy to understand helps maintain your beat and connection with the audience.

Well-laid-out and easy-to-follow slides also show the audience you know what you're doing and that you care about making good use of their time. That alone helps build a strong connection. You don't need PowerPoint to connect with the audience, but it's a strong tool I advise speakers to use whenever they can.

Final PowerPoint Tips

Set up early. If you're going to use PowerPoint and a projector with your computer, you and whoever is the master of the audio-visual stuff should be the first people in the room. It's difficult to look cool, confident, and professional in front of an audience while hunched over, hooking up the computer to the projector, praying there's an ounce of truth to the words, "I'm waiting for this to boot up. It will be just a minute." Feeling that trickle of sweat working its way down the nape of your neck isn't a real confidence builder. Arrive early and make sure the projector and the computer are working properly and that the image looks clean and clear when it's projected. If not, stop everything and get some help from an AV guru. From my experience, those guys love helping the technically challenged. Once things look great, stand next to the projector, look directly at the screen, and flip through your slides, resting a second or two on each one. This is like going through the playbook, or music sheet (whatever!) one final time. It's a good tool to get psyched up. Once you've gone through all the slides, have a glass of iced tea and relax. You're ready to be great.

Get a clicker. You'll definitely look cooler than Colin Farrell when you've got one of those little wireless clickers in your hand, advancing the slides even though you are across the room. This isn't mandatory, but for less than $50 it sure does make you look and feel cool, composed, and in charge. It beats the heck out of dashing back to the computer and hitting the space bar every time you change slides. Ask the clerk at the electronics store for a wireless remote for your PowerPoint presentation. There are several different models with a transmitter that plugs right into the USB port on your laptop. Plug it in and go through your slides with ease. Practice first (chapter 9 will harp on this) and prepare to enter the world of the suave.

Action items for your next presentation:

1. If you aren't familiar with PowerPoint, try it out. It's not hard to learn.
2. Create your presentation template. These sixteen slides will be your road map to connecting with the audience.
3. Make the slides with the motto "Less is more."
4. Schedule time now to get to your presentation room early to set up.

6

Numbers Are Not Your Friends— Use Them Sparingly

- Numbers can draw the audience away from your power sound bite and from your presentation.
- Too many numbers create a permanent disconnection between you and your audience.
- When you delete numbers and replace them with vivid supporting statements, you'll improve your presentations.
- You're going to need *some* numbers to tell your story. Use them correctly to support your power sound bite.

The fewer the numbers in your next presentation, the better off you and the audience will be. So we're going to spend this chapter weaning you off numbers, while showing you how to make the numbers you keep meaningful to your audience and helpful to your presentation.

Please don't discount this chapter as the tweedy raving of some touchy-feely humanities major who's frightened to get down to brass tacks. I love the idea of brass tacks, though I'm not sure I've literally ever seen them, let alone gotten down to them. You do need numbers, but not nearly as many as in most presentations. Because everyone processes numbers and their meanings at different speeds, numbers can be jarring speed bumps in your road to connecting with the audience. Numbers can be cold and distracting, thereby destroying hard-won connections with audiences. Using number after number is the easy way out for presenters who don't want to commit to the work it takes to help the audience connect to their power sound bites. When you are willing to work on your stories, you'll voluntarily relinquish your frightened tight grasp of digits and percentages.

Even though I got a "D" in trigonometry in my junior year of high school, I'm not anti-numbers or anti-math. I like reading the financial statements of companies I follow and enjoy the columns in the *Wall Street Journal* that feature economic indicators. Though my math skills dissuaded me from an academic path leaning toward public accounting, I fully understand the relationship among sales, gross margin, fixed costs, and profitability.

I'm a big fan of the software Excel and I use it almost every workday. I especially enjoy watching the program handle a lot of the formulas that so plagued me in high school. I'm thrilled that the software lets me change one number or one variable in the row, which instantly changes other results and formulas all over the spreadsheet.

Numbers are helpful, and I agree with the language that we use to describe how we work with numbers.

- Numbers need to be *pored over*.
- Numbers need to be *tweaked*.
- Numbers need to be *interpreted*.
- Numbers need to be *adjusted*.
- Numbers need to be *reworked*.

Numbers need to be understood. But here's the catch, as well as the point of this chapter. We all interact with numbers at different speeds that swing wildly from one audience member to another.

With my "D" in trigonometry I couldn't see, interpret, or find significant relationships between numbers as quickly as the class know-it-alls who were garnering easy "A's" with a bored sigh and a flatulent smile, saying they were really looking forward to calculus next year.

This is why large amounts of numbers and formulas don't work well as a part of any presentation. All people do math in their heads, everyone interprets numbers at different speeds. Even smart math people vary in how quickly they can figure out numbers on the fly.

It does not matter how beautiful, elegant, and simply awesome the PowerPoint graph on the screen may be. When the speaker points to it and says, "Well, it's obvious that sales projections in Q2 of 7,856 units on average in each of our six domestic territories compared with Q3 projections of 6,948 units on average for those same six domestic territories will lead to a gross margin reduction of 22.5 percent in the fourth quarter," my response is usually, "Do what now? The only thing that's obvious is that this is way too much for me to follow."

A cavalcade of numbers and their relationships to each other are far more welcome on computer screens, printed reports, or spreadsheets than when they're projected on a screen and spoken to captured groups of colleagues. Individuals get more meaning out of numbers when they can make the most of them at their own speed. The speaker may be going too slow or too fast, which is why you should know that number after number bogs down presentations. Numbers are most meaningful when they are seen, reviewed, and understood in a quiet environment, not heard in a conference room. Keep numbers to a minimum and your presentation will be stronger. Make sure when you include a number, you're sure it will have meaning to the audience that you can immediately explain.

You may think I'm wrong, and may hasten to argue, "Well, you don't know my board. This isn't some touchy-feely group. They want cold, hard facts, not 'Kumbayah' around a campfire. They want numbers plain and simple. The more the better, Mr. Birkenstock-wearing–herbal tea lover." You are right (except for the "Birkenstock" thing), but I want you to do it anyway. I agree: Your boss, your board, your customer, your banker, your investors all want numbers. So give them what they want, and don't think I want you to deny them those numbers. Go ahead and deliver all the numbers on clean documents in a crisp manila folder, in an e-mail with lots of attachments, or in fancy printed presentations with a clear plastic cover. Give them all kinds of comparative numbers they can see and study at their own pace. Give them tons of numbers they can look at from the privacy of their own desk, or corner table during an afternoon coffee break at Starbucks.

Numbers work best and are of the most benefit when they are seen, not heard. When your vocal chords are clanging together, standing in front of those "numbers only" guys, keep to a minimum the numbers that spill out of your mouth. Instead, learn to talk about what the numbers mean to everyone in the room. I'm going to show you how to do that and still keep the numbers guys thinking you are brilliant. Numbers take away from the presentation experience and hurt your power sound bite, hurt your supporting sentences, and kill your stories. The fewer the numbers the speaker relies on, the better the connection with the audience. I am not proclaiming complete numbers cleaning or number abstinence, but do not rely on numbers to create a lasting connection with your audience.

Here's why numbers don't help you, why too many (more than a couple per presentation) can hurt you, and why even the most cold-hearted men and women who always just want to get down to brass tacks—un-emotive executives with ice water in their veins—will be happy you left most of the numbers behind.

The most critical conversations and discussions of your life have not involved numbers. Not just my life, but your life, everybody's life. Critical, important, landmark discussions just don't sound right if someone is repeatedly throwing out numbers. That tells me numbers aren't really that critical. They're to be understood, they're to be taken into consideration. But presentations and conversations are most intense when they focus on what the numbers mean, not the numbers themselves. Great presenters know that and shy away from using too many numbers. Let's go through some typical life scenarios.

High School Scenario

The scene: The corridors of your high school
The topic: The upcoming prom

The normal conversation without numbers:

Jackie, I've come to the conclusion that every time I'm with you I feel great. You're smart, you make me laugh, and I find myself thinking about you all day long. I like you and I wanted to know if you would go to the prom with me.

The silly conversation with numbers:

Jackie, 95 percent of the time I'm with you, I feel great. You got a 1,275 on the SAT, which is a very strong score, good enough for most top-notch state schools, though hardly Ivy League mate-

rial, which demands upward of 1,500. That's okay with me, though. Statistically, according to the universe of high school seniors, you're still pretty smart. Six times last week you made me laugh. I found myself thinking about you approximately 5.5 times each conscious hour of the day. This numerical analysis leads me to the conclusion that I like you and I wanted to know if you would go to the prom with me.

College Graduation Dinner Scenario

The scene: The nice restaurant near campus
The topic: Thanks and gratitude

The normal conversation without numbers:

Mom and Dad, thank you for giving me a wonderful college experience. I know it was expensive to send me out of state, and that you had to work harder and longer, as well as make sacrifices to allow me to study my major here. I want you to know I'll never forget it. Your support and your love mean the world to me. I promise to make good on your investment in me, and to carry on the tradition by providing my children with a great education.

The silly conversation with numbers:

Mom and Dad, thank you for giving me a wonderful college experience. I know it cost $92,528, spread out over sixteen aca-

demic quarters. Mom, you had to increase your billable hours at the accounting firm by 16 percent over the last three years, and Dad, you had to sink 78 percent of your after-tax bonus into my college fund. Also, I know that last summer you replaced a $9,600 trip to Tuscany with a $1,900 trip to the Wisconsin Dells. Your support and your love mean the world to me. I promise to be making a solid six figures by the time I'm twenty-nine and to carry on the tradition by providing my children with a great education. Of course, with an estimated yearly inflation rate of 3.2 percent and taking into account the future value of present dollars, I'll be spending a lot more than you did . . . 43.8 percent more to be exact. Just the same, thanks.

These are exaggerated examples, but I bet we all know people who lean toward this type of precise numerical communication. Numbers, though accurate, do not help the speaker in any of these slices of life. They hurt the communication process because they focus on stats, not the PSB and the supporting statements. Too many numbers in a presentation create a chill in the air and a deadening of the emotion in a meeting. Here are my specific reasons for opposing a reliance on numbers.

Numbers Are Not Pleasant or Reassuring

I've already established my lack of strength when it comes to math, but I know there's lots of numbers out there: zillions, quadrillions, who knows? It's amazing how few of them sound good when you're talking. Finally, if you're going to use a number, determine whether it works well as the answer to a question, or if it sounds obvious and self-serving.

Even those numbers that sound good, sound weird out loud. Here are some examples:

MANUFACTURING ENVIRONMENT: TALKING TO YOUR PRODUCTION TEAM

Numbers-based weak power sound bite: *I don't want a single down-time report this month to hit my desk. Not one.*

Strong power sound bite without numbers: *I want us to be up, running, and productive every minute you're here, full steam ahead. Our customers and our prosperity depend on it.*

Critique: "Productive every minute" is stronger than "not a single down-time report."

Ridiculous question test: How many times do you want the line to stop because of production failures? (Answer: zero)

SALES ENVIRONMENT: A SHORT-LIST PRESENTATION

Numbers-based weak power sound bite: *I know after hearing the six presentations you'll sit through today, you'll rank our team number one.*

Strong power sound bite without numbers: *I know you've got a long day ahead, and you will hear from some great teams. When the day is over, I know you'll want us as your partner as you move your company forward.*

Sounds better in a presentation lesson: "Your partner" is stronger than "number one."

Ridiculous question test: Where do you want your customers to rank your company after a day-long series of presentations from you and your competitors? (Answer: number one)

IT/MIS ENVIRONMENT

Numbers-based weak power sound bite: *Guys, this is important. I'll tolerate no bugs, I mean zero, as soon as we go live with this new application. I'm not kidding. If I get even a single call from a customer who gets a wrong shipment, I'm going to send them to you.*

Strong power sound bite without numbers: *The software has to work flawlessly from the moment we go live. I want our customers happy, not calling me to complain.*

Sounds better in a presentation lesson: "Work flawlessly" is stronger than "I mean zero."

Ridiculous question test: How many incorrect orders do you want shipped to your customers after transitioning your company to new supply chain software? (Answer: zero)

HUMAN RESOURCES ENVIRONMENT

Numbers-based weak power sound bite: *We have to be careful how we treat our employees who are over fifty years old. Last year we had three age-discrimination lawsuits threatened. I want to cut that number to zero if possible.*

Strong power sound bite without numbers: *We have to treat all our employees with respect and dignity, whether they just entered the workforce or have enjoyed a long career already. I want our mature workers to feel this is a great place to work so that they will tell their friends and others in the community. The age-discrimination lawsuits we saw last year tell me we're doing a lousy job.*

Sounds better in a presentation lesson: "great place to work" is stronger than "three age-discrimination law-suits."

Ridiculous question: How many age-discrimination lawsuits do you want coming across your desk this year? (Answer: zero)

MARKETING ENVIRONMENT

Numbers-based weak power sound bite: *I want to be number one in our category.*

Strong power sound bite without numbers: *When our customers have a choice, I want them picking us, their old friend, time after time.*

Sounds better in a presentation lesson: "Picking us, their old friend" is stronger than "number one."

Ridiculous question: What place do you want to be in after a brand recognition survey is conducted among consumers? (Answer: first place)

Every one of these examples demonstrates the weakness of relying on numbers when you're speaking to a group. A speaker who relies on numbers sounds unimaginative and weak, spouting the corporate or tough-guy line. Like most flaws in presentations, using numbers isn't a capital offense. It's just another flaw that distances and bores listeners, leaving them with an impression of you that is less favorable than before you began speaking.

Percentages Are the Worst Numbers

Percentages rarely work to your advantage, whether you're in front of six people or six hundred. Once you mention a percentage, you're begging the audience to stop listening to you and do the reverse math. Or even worse, you're calling the integrity of you or your company into question. Percentages are meant to be seen and not heard! They do not work to your advantage, and you should cut as many as possible from your presentation. As soon as you mention a percentage, all of the attention leaves your power sound bite and moves to numerical calculations about the percentage you just mentioned.

Here's how mentioning a percentage works to your disadvantage.

I'm a nervous flyer, despite flying frequently to various coaching assignments. Even though you are supposedly safer in a commercial aircraft than in your own car, I still feel the urge to shake like a child each time my plane takes off. Here's what really brings on the fear and loathing: After takeoff, the captain comes on the intercom and says, "Ladies and Gentlemen, we've reached our cruising altitude of thirty-two thousand feet. This is normally the time when I'd turn off the seat belt sign and allow you to move comfortably about the cabin. However, ATC [air traffic control] has advised us of some turbulence in the air ahead. So, I'm going to keep that seat belt light illuminated. We're going to hit quite a few light bumps in the next few minutes, so I'd like the flight attendants to stow their carts and buckle up as well. Hey, we know you have a choice when you fly, thanks for choosing us. We'll be checking in with you in a few minutes."

While I'm freaking out, with my luck there would be an airline pilot, in full pilot garb, sitting across the aisle from me. With a reassuring touch on the arm he might say, "Hey, fella, I can see you're upset. I want to tell you, you can start to relax. I personally know the guy flying this baby. When he hits turbulence, even severe bumps like we're going through, 99 percent of the time, he comes out of it just fine. So try to calm down."

Calm down! Even a mathematic moron like me can do those numbers. What if this is his one hundredth time hitting air like this? Is my life insurance paid up? Did I tell my kids I love them today? Do I have time to listen to "Aqualung" one last time on my iPod on the way down?

Every time you mention a percentage, you're asking the audience to do reverse math and ask, "Gee, couldn't we do better?" No matter what percentage you mention to your boss or your banker or your customer, everyone will do the reverse math and wonder how you're going to improve it. Percentages beg the audience to leave you, go off in their own mathematical world, and start to run different "what ifs."

Don't think 100 percent gets you off the hook either. The items you should be able to hit 100 percent on aren't things you should have to mention or draw attention to. Here's what I mean.

To your spouse: *Honey, I had a great business trip this week. I missed you a bunch and I gotta tell you I was 100 percent faithful to you this week! Not a single misstep! Now, gimme a big kiss.*

To your boss: *I know you're concerned about pilfering in the supply room, but 100 percent of the time I've left work, I've done so without a single legal pad or printer cartridge that I didn't absolutely need.*

To your employees: *Well, it being the fifteenth at the end of the week, we all know payroll is going to hit the corporate bank account. I'm here to tell you this week there's a 100 percent chance your checks will clear on Friday.*

Numbers Meant to Sound Impressive Sound Silly

If you use a number as the indication of an accomplishment, you're on weak ground. It shows you are lazy and not working hard enough to describe to the audience the value of your power sound bite. You've reduced it to a number. How demeaning! Your PSB deserves better. If you're using numbers to constantly prop up your points, it's as if you're working hard to convince the audience of something you may not believe in yourself. Let's go to the examples.

Example: *Jill is the right candidate for our international marketing position. She combines the perfect mix of Fortune 500 marketing expertise and the understanding of a broad array of business issues.*

Weak supporting statement using numbers: *We have to keep in mind that despite the fact Jill has little experience in our industry, she does speak eight foreign languages, all fluently.*

Unspoken sarcasm from the audience: *Rats, I was hoping for someone with nine foreign languages. How about twelve languages, conversational, not fluent? Next candidate!*

Strong supporting statement without numbers: *We have to keep in mind that despite the fact Jill has little experience in our industry, she's got a great command of foreign languages. That's very important to our efforts. Imagine the leg-up we'll have over our competition when she can speak German to our customers in Bonn, and Portuguese in São Paulo. They'll know we're going the extra mile to give them great service when she can ask them about their vacations or their kids in their own language.*

The last statement calls for the presenter to put more thought into the supporting statement.

Burning question: What the heck am I supposed to do with all the numbers in my presentation for next Tuesday?

First off, stop hyperventilating. You don't have to dump them all to keep your audience interested. But make sure when you focus on throwing out a number, you're being considerate of the audience. Work hard to support your PSB in the best way possible instead of the easiest way for you. Throwing in a ton of numbers to support your power sound bite makes things easier for you but harder for your audience.

Use numbers if you're convinced the presentation continues to be meaningful and helpful to the audience. Just make sure the audience understands the meaning of the numbers and the meaning of your power sound bite. Here's a quick tip: Every time you use a number, add the rejoinder "which means." That will cue you to give your thoughts on why the number is important to your PSB. Here's how it works.

Example: *Domestic sales were down 11 percent in the last quarter, which means our backlog is shrinking and we're not going to have any work to do if we don't pick up the pace. We need to start sweating.*

Example: *Our main customers are now ordering 11,400 pieces a month. That's up from 6,300 last year, which means we're doing a great job for them. Now we need to study our labor costs to make sure we're producing every piece with high quality, while keeping our profits up. This is a good problem to have!*

If you're a numbers junkie, take heart. You can do this. It's easier than weaning yourself off nicotine, caffeine, or *I love the 80s* on VH1. You will realize you have fully kicked the numbers habit once you enjoy all those pats on the back after your "number light" presentation. Every time you make a presentation that's "light" on numbers, your audience will be appreciative.

Action items for your next presentation:

1. Realize that numbers are not what the audience is looking for.
2. Study every number in your presentation and make sure it's there for a good reason, not just because it makes you think you sound smart or thorough.
3. Get rid of numbers by substituting stronger, more meaningful action words.
4. If you leave some numbers in (and it's okay if you do), make sure you tack on the two words "which means" that will explain their relevance to the audience.

Dump as many numbers from your presentation as possible.

Keep the research, the homework, the insight, the examples, just deliver them without the digits. Your presentation will still all add up to more success for you.

Finally, there's a perfect cinematic example of the meaningless value of numbers in a single scene from the 1983 classic *This Is Spinal Tap*. My advice: Rent it or buy it immediately, then fast-forward to the scene where Spinal Tap lead guitarist Nigel Tufnel (Christopher Guest) is proudly displaying his stage guitars and amplifiers to rock-film documentarian Marti DiBergi (Rob Reiner). I'm not going to ruin this for you, but if you watch this family-friendly scene you'll reap the following benefits:

◆ You'll get a good laugh.
◆ You'll understand my contention that numbers by themselves have no meaning.
◆ The next time someone says under their breath, "This one goes to eleven" (it happens more than you know!) and you get the joke, you'll realize you've inadvertently joined a widespread subculture.
◆ You'll have a hard time saying the numbers ten or eleven (by themselves) with a straight face.

7

Friends Don't Let Friends Say "Basically"—Eliminate Disconnection Expressions

WHAT YOU WILL LEARN FROM THIS CHAPTER:

- Seemingly harmless words and expressions can turn the audience against you.
- What the words and expressions are.
- How you can replace them with words and expressions that help instead of hurt you.

This is the outpatient surgery section of *Presentation S.O.S.* I'm going to show you presentation warts and bunions you've never seen before and how to excise them from your next talk. You probably don't even recognize these presentation blemishes, but they've been making your presentations and overall communications unpleasant and sometimes downright ugly for years. No more! It's time to cut the offending presentation growths out, quickly and efficiently. If this is too invasive a procedure, let's say we're going to make sure we get the broccoli out from between your teeth.

Either way, to continue with the grooming and hygiene motif, we're going to make your presentation teeth sparkle and your presentation skin clear as we get rid of the presentation toxins and disturbing growths you didn't even know you had.

Dump these presentation demons and your presentation will be more uplifting and strike a stronger connection with the audience. It's going to take as much work as creating your power sound bite or painting a picture, because these presentation killers are deeply ingrained. They're with us every day, all day. Like cockroaches, they survive in all environments: boardroom, conference room, lunchroom, boiler room. But they never have to leave your mouth. You're in control and can keep the Beelzebubs of babble at bay with concentration and focus.

We've all sat through presentations where the speaker sends a conflicting signal to the audience: "I want my messages to connect with you, but at the same time, I'm using words and expressions that will push you away. You see, I just don't know how to act." Now, you've never walked away from a presentation like this with hurt feelings, saying, "Wow, that was passive-aggressive. What a weasel!" Instead, you walk away saying, "That just wasn't a very good use of my time. I didn't connect with her at all." There's tons of dysfunction going on here. The speaker doesn't want to push the audience away; the audience doesn't want to leave the room feeling slighted.

This chapter will help you understand the subtle, ever-present "relationship damaging" words that you can identify and dismiss from your next presentation. Now (reassuring voice), let's move on with the healing, remove the passive-aggressive behavior, and start functioning normally. Just don't expect a group hug at the end.

I've been asking you to make addition after addition to your presentation. Now it's time to start subtracting.

Connecting with an audience is a two-step process. You've got to say things that connect, or bring the audience closer to you; then, you must dump the seemingly harmless and overused expressions that disconnect or push the audience away.

So many speakers throw up roadblocks to presentation success with ridiculous, weak, and obnoxious expressions that kill the potential beauty of the presentation experience. You wouldn't think of ruining a first meeting with the sentence, "I really like those slacks you're wearing. Did they fit when you bought them?" Why would anyone deliver subtle yet insulting, demeaning, and patronizing comments? Speakers do it all the time, all day every day. "They" (you know them) do it because everybody else does, and you're just repeating what you hear. It's more of that audience abuse.

Audiences have become so deadened to this abuse that it may not even register at a conscious level. But every time you use a "presentation killer," you're pushing the audience away. Do it more than a few times and you'll ruin the moment. No euphoria, no intense bonding, just weak and merely polite, luke-warm applause.

I'm going to go through my list of presentation killers. These are words and expressions that you'll hear in everyday presentations and conversations. Distressingly, you'll even hear them on TV; you'll hear them on the radio, from well-paid, top-of-the-ladder, professional communicators.

If you can eliminate these tiresome words, everything you say will sound better: your PSB, your supporting statements, your entire presentation. If you can eliminate them from every-day conversation, your colleagues, family, and friends will be amazed. You'll sound more confident, poised, and strong. Getting rid of presentation killers is worthwhile, but it takes diligence. Nobody likes a passive-aggressive, yet people regularly have to tolerate speakers who deliver lots of passive-aggressive terms and phrases. Not you, though!

Chances are you'll agree, "Yeah, I hate it when someone says that, too." But my experience in running thousands of work-shops and coaching sessions is that even though you'll agree with me, getting rid of the deadly words and expressions will be a challenge. They're so deeply ingrained, so much a part of this bizarre corporate professional nano-speak that's repeated like clockwork, the dastardly words and expressions have become painfully acceptable. Most audience members are so used to hearing presentation killers they don't even flinch when they hear them in meeting after meeting. Mild disappointment registers somewhere deep inside every audience member, reminding them why they don't enjoy most presentations or meetings.

How sad. When you develop your presentation, you should be working to astound, to enlighten, or at least to be helpful. When you use presentation killers, your work goes down the drain and you slip into instant mediocrity. That means we're going to have to work hard to dispel the presentation villains.

Wimpy Qualifiers and Modifiers

These are the words and phrases that mediocre communicators use to buffer, soften, and eventually nullify their ideas.

> *As far as I know . . .*
> *Probably . . .*
> *For the most part . . .*
> *Sort of . . .*
> *Pretty much . . .*

This is not a complete list of wimpy qualifiers and modifiers that kill presentations, but it's a great starting place. The weak communicator uses them for one of three reasons:

1. They have an ongoing, never-ending bad habit of using evasive words or expressions, even when they're trying to be direct.

2. They don't want to be held to their ideas should something go wrong.
3. They want to mask their convictions.

Sometimes they're able to hit all three in the same speech: a
wimpy triple! One, two, or all three—it still adds up to a bad
performance. No power sound bites or supporting statements
or stories are made better by these words.

Here's the "wimp-out" test. If you aren't sure of yourself
and want to qualify the thoughts in your next presentation, see
whether the same expression would do damage in your personal life. Let's go through some scenarios.

- On your wedding day, at the front of the congrega-
  tion, staring at your beloved and responding to the
  big question: *I do, as far as I know . . .*
- On the night of your teenager's first prom, impart-
  ing your final instructions: *You probably shouldn't
  drink alcohol or use drugs before, during, or after the
  prom tonight.*
- At a memorial service for a dear friend: *He was for
  the most part the type of person every single one of us
  could turn to in times of need.*
- As you toast your significant other during an
  anniversary dinner: *I sort of think you are my soul
  mate. I'm sort of glad I found you.*
- At a seventy-fifth birthday party for a parent: *I am
  pretty much proud to tell everyone that you're my
  mother.*

These wimpy qualifiers and modifiers all sound ridiculous and silly for the same reason. They reduce the speaker's commitment during serious and heartfelt moments, making the statements become hurtful instead of helpful. That's exactly what happens when you use them in a presentation, even when there's far less emotion on the line. Your lack of backbone in saying, "We should hit our projections, as far as I know," won't hurt any feelings in the room. It will hurt your reputation as a strong and confident colleague, though. By using these words, you're qualifying and covering yourself from the statement, just in case things don't go as planned. That's the opposite of strong, bold, and direct, and it makes the audience feel uncomfortable and disconnected.

I don't care what genre or time period you pick, try to find lyrics to a musical hit with this kind of cautionary tone. These just don't have the same punch as the original.

"I did it my way, *for the most part.*"

"When you're rockin' and a rollin' and you *sort of* hear your mamma call."

"She's a Black Magic Woman, *as far as I know.*"

"Walk, *pretty much*, this way."

"I'm *probably* talkin' 'bout my generation."

Frank Sinatra, Little Richard, Carlos Santana, Steven Tyler, and Pete Townshend knew memorable and moving lyrics should not include hesitancy or appeasement, or display any concern that you might be wrong about your ideas.

Qualifiers and modifiers show that you're not sure what you're saying, or that you're unwilling to stand behind it. Speakers use qualifiers when they want wiggle room, a fudge factor. They aren't willing to put their ideas or their backsides on the line.

That's the opposite of what the audience is looking for in a presentation experience. They want strength, they want power, they want ideas and plans they can follow. It's uninspiring to listen to someone who's always qualifying their thoughts. That means the speaker wants to keep that qualifier to use later in the future: "Well, I didn't promise we'd hit our sales goals, I said we would, 'as far as I know.'" The audience smells the lack of conviction with every backpedal. Who thinks highly of the colleague who's always, desperately trying to limit liability for their ideas?

What If You Aren't Sure?

You can use strong, powerful statements without telling the audience to bet their life savings on your recommendations. There are many ways to appear strong and vibrant without being cocky, overly authoritative, or unrealistic. Here are some qualifying statements that include qualifiers that sound strong and help maintain a connection with the audience:

- *Based on our performance the last two quarters and our new products, this is a likely pattern for our sales growth. We're going to be moving forward.*

- *I don't know yet if we'll be working the day after Thanksgiving this year. But I can tell you this. If our orders keep increasing through the early fall the way they have during the last summer, I'll see you bright and early that Friday, with a turkey sandwich in a lunch bag with a little Tupperware thing filled with cranberry sauce. We're lucky to have customers who like our unique products. We're having a good year.*
- *Both applicants are strong, and it's a shame we only have the budget for one of them. My homework tells me we'll need Glenda's financial analysis skills more than Eric's marketing expertise as soon as we ramp up overseas operations. I vote for Glenda, but will welcome Eric if the team wants to go the other way.*

Be strong and direct, and connect with the audience by surgically removing all wimpy qualifiers and modifiers from your next presentation.

Basically, "Basically" Has No Place in Your Vocabulary

I have strong negative feelings about the word "basically." It's a close relative of the dreaded backpedaling modifiers, but it does so much damage that it deserves its own section.

"Basically" is a subtle and effective way of telling everyone that you're brighter, sharper, and quicker on the uptake than they are. But, because you are kindhearted, you're going to take pity on the simpletons gaping at you with drooling, slightly open mouths, and lend them a hand. Think that's too harsh? The word is strong and negative. After all, you're the one announcing that you're going to the trouble of making your complex ideas, thoughts, and power sound bites "basic." And you're doing it just for them!

At a party or at a networking event, I may ask a new acquaintance what they do for a living. If they start the explanation with, "Well, basically," I shut down completely. It's all I can do not to raise the palm of my hand up violently in front of them ("talk to the hand") and interrupt them with, "Now wait just a minute here, buster! My dad worked nights to put me through graduate school, where I finished first in my class. You don't have to make anything 'basic.' You can dispense with the version for dum-dums and give me the difficult explanation. Let's see if someone you think is a moron can handle it." Fortunately, one of the lobes of my brain still houses the self-control synapse, and I burn quietly and try to enjoy the party.

Every time you use the word "basically" you're telling the audience that you are wiser, smarter than they are. The audience won't go along with that, but the inkling crops up that you are conceited and condescending. This "basically" insult is subtle, just under the radar, and hurts every speaker. "Basically" is a miserable word to use if your goal is to connect with the audience. If you want to put them down, it's a great choice.

Yet "basically" seems to be gaining in popularity in our culture, month by month. It's the mocha latte of adverbs. It hurts my ears every time I hear it, and unfortunately, that's a lot. Even communication superstars, like Katie and Matt on the *Today* show, wonderful role models for telling stories and developing power sound bites, fall into the "basically" abyss almost every morning. Why the popularity of such a worthless, meaningless word?

Let's you and I stop it right now and realize "basically" has little value, unless you intend to demean your audience. "Basically" is a substitute for a pause, a breath, a half second of quiet that's so much more effective. Every time you hear the word "basically," imagine how the comment would be better if there was just a beat of silence replacing it. The result is a sentence that's more direct, more pleasant to the ear, and more confident sounding.

"Essentially" and "primarily" are not good end runs around "basically." Dump those as well. While you're at it, get rid of "simply put . . ." No one wants to be told you have to make it simple for them.

When You Have to Say You're Honest, They Start to Wonder

When you tell the audience "honestly," you throw pallor of doubt over your entire presentation. "Honestly" means you are *now* being honest. Why do you have to say this right now, at the beginning of this sentence or thought? Does that mean all the preceding ideas and concepts are dishonest, disingenuous, and filled with falsehoods? Is your reputation for telling scurrilous lies so widespread that you feel the need to say to the audience,

"At this moment, I have to let you know, I'm being honest with you." When you go to the trouble to highlight a single statement as honest, you cast doubt on all the other statements.

The negative vibes under-the-radar thing is starting to work here, as you give a mild unpleasant jolt to the audience, disrupting your connection. They dampen the positives of the presentation experience, like an overturned glass of water in your lap in the middle of a delicious meal at a nice restaurant. The audience may forgive or overlook a single "honestly" if you're lucky. Say "honestly" several times during your talk and you'll ruin all connections while the audience giggles to themselves saying, "Yeah, well thanks for being honest for once in your life."

There's a huge irony here. "Honestly" and its evil cousins "frankly" and "to tell you the truth" aren't attempts to call attention to the fact that this sentence or thought or story is filled with integrity, unlike the other falsehoods that preceded it. Instead, the "honesty" trio is the result, as usual, of the speaker taking the easy way out and not working hard enough. The "honesty" trio usually is a substitute for:

- *This is important.*
- *This is serious.*
- *I'm passionate about this.*
- *This is something I don't want to leave the room.*
- *I care about this and I want you to as well.*

All of these take slightly more work and a more deliberate thought process to spit out during a presentation. "Honestly" follows "basically" and the backpedaling modifiers as words and expressions that hurt the presentation experience, but everyone seems to tolerate and then repeat. Just say "no" to the "honesty" trio. No end runs with "candidly" either. It may be more elegant, but it's still a bad choice.

Repetition Is Good—Just Don't Call Attention to It

If you can repeat your power sound bite every few minutes of your presentation, you maintain your connection with the audience. When you remind the audience you're repeating your PSB, you break that connection. Repeating the power sound bite bestows cadence and rhythm and gives the room energy. Drawing attention to your repetition shatters that cadence and ruins the positive vibes.

That means you need to excise the phrases "As I said before . . ." and "As I mentioned . . ." The audience doesn't need to be reminded you said this two or three minutes ago. The speaker who says, "as I said before" appears to be admonishing the audience or worse, implying the dullards in the audience need the repetition. When I hear, "let me repeat" coming from the speaker's lips, I hear this:

- *Let me repeat this for you, Mark, since you obviously weren't listening the first time.*
- *As I said before, Mark, you meandering incompetent.*

More abounding irony, because that's never what the speaker intends to communicate. These speakers are doing nothing more than regressing to a hyperventilating eighth grader at the podium for the first time in speech class, who keeps saying, "Okay, ah, okay, um, okay." "As I said before" is a way for insecure speakers to verbally pat themselves on the back for reassurance: "I'm on solid ground here, I've said this before. This is okay." There's no reason to say it. Just repeat your PSB without drawing attention to it.

The only time "as I said before" or "let me repeat" is a direct form of communication is when you're angry and trying to start an argument. Clearly, unless you're interested in creating tension, anger, and resentment (I personally have succeeded at all three), do not mention that you've said something before. Just say it again.

The presentation killers, warts, bunions are all around, all day, every day. Cut them out, be vigilant. Do not let them return. Success is in sight.

Action items for your next presentation:

1. Realize the audience can turn against you unless you eliminate harmful words and expressions from your presentation.

2. Become conscious of your everyday use of backpedaling modifiers, "basically," the "honesty" trio, and repeating and calling attention to it.

3. Place a bounty on these words: Offer to pay your coworkers, your kids, or your significant others a dollar every time "basically" or one of the other offenders leaves your

lips. By the time you've opened your wallet and handed out your fifth dollar bill to your nine-year-old, you should be cured.

4. Be glad when you hear one of these presentation blasphemies coming from someone else, with the self-assured knowledge that you now know better!

8

Wrap Up with a Bang:
Your Power Close,
Winning the Q&A Battle, and
Making the Most of the Accolades

- How to develop a power close that will work every time.
- How to develop a second, more adventurous power close.
- How to navigate the minefield of questions and come out a winner.
- How to turn those pats on the back into personal equity.

You can see the presentation finish line ahead and you realize that you're going to win. You can now see and feel the audience connecting with you. They're leaning forward in their chairs. You see the genuine smiles and even hear laughter at the clever parts; you can just feel it's real laughter, not the polite or sympathetic chuckle or two. When you hit your power sound bite for the fifth, sixth, and seventh time as you roar toward the conclusion, you see them nodding slightly. Perhaps they're even giving you the unabashed, out-and-out "You're really doing well" up-and-down nods. They feel the impact of your message. They understand. They're on your side! This feels good. The "mojo is rising." You find yourself wondering, perhaps for the first time ever, when can I do it again?

This chapter is about wrapping up your presentation so well, they *will* ask you again, maybe even before you walk out the door. There's a game plan to ending strong, to staying strong during questions, even pesky questions, and then making the most of the praise others are heaping upon you. Develop and deliver a power close and you will leave them wanting more—of your ideas, of your brains, of your energy.

The "Repetition" Power Close: Safe and Strong

It's effective and reliable to close your presentation with a carefully timed repetition of your power sound bite and supporting statements. Yikes! This smacks of "their" old chestnut: *Tell them what you're going to tell them. Tell them. Tell them what you told them.* "They" are right, so let's take advantage of it. This is a very strong approach that will help maintain your connection with the audience.

When you wrap up your presentation with a precise rundown of what you've done in the last fifteen or thirty minutes, you're accomplishing a lot.

- You're repeating your power sound bite.
- You're supporting your power sound bite by repeating supporting statements.
- You're showing the audience that you made good on the unspoken promise, to make good use of their time.

This is not a daring or dramatic close (I'll give you one of those in a few pages), but it works and builds your confidence as you wrap up. The repetition close works to your strongest advantage when you can get your game face on, pump up your energy level, and propel through your final sentences with a rhythm. It's the only time when you need to point out the fact you said something before. Let's go "back, back, back, back" as ESPN's Chris Berman would say, to chapter 2 (the one about creating the power sound bite) and see how this plays out. The highlights show what you need to add to create your power close. I've reworded the supporting statements for a stronger beat, but have not added any new ideas or concepts.

- I told you when I started *that you're the best team in the region. You're the ones who will show everyone else how to achieve superior results. I'm delighted and honored to lead you in your efforts.*

- I've asked you to change *the way we service our customers, and track the success of each product in our line, and put an end to our county-by-county sales tracking system.*
- I've asked you to learn some new software *to accept and then master a new customer's database system that our headquarters has invested in.*
- I've asked you to accept a management change and to *congratulate and support Jennifer, who I am now promoting to regional district supervisor.*

The repetition close is strong, it's clear, and it creates rhythm in the room and continues a series of connections with the audience. It's a safe, sure way to finish every presentation.

The "Story" Power Close: More Work, More Impact

If you're feeling a bit saucy, then consider going one step further than the repetition power close. The "story" power close asks you to introduce a new element all the way at the end of the presentation. This takes some work and more boldness on your part. It's worth it, especially as you strengthen your presentation delivery muscles and have the time and energy to end with a memorable finale.

Here's how it works. After you're done providing all the data and backup to your final supporting statement for your

PSB, pause and take a nice deep breath. Then, as if to cue yourself and the audience to get in the storytelling mode, use these words: *"I'd like to share a story with you . . ."* or, *"I'd like to paint a picture for you . . ."*

Now, you're ready to launch into a powerful story or example that will describe and re-emphasize the benefits of your power sound bite and all your supporting documents. This new story can be real or imagined, in the future, in the past. It can be about someone you've already mentioned, or it can be about someone the audience is hearing about for the first time. It can be about a relative, a customer, a friend, someone you don't know. But make this story about someone you can see in your mind. This person and his or her story will give you a chance to weave in your PSB and supporting statements and charge them with greater emotion.

The goal is to have your audience imagining or seeing your power sound bite in action, to see it come alive. I believe this is the strongest end for any presentation and tends to leave the audience wishing the talk could go on. Let's take a look at it in action using our familiar PSB. The highlighted power sound bite comes all the way at the end, in the story close.

Let me tell you a story about a phone call I look forward to receiving next year at this time. The call is from Gil in Wilkes-Barre, our largest customer in Pennsylvania, and it's a good phone call. He's picked up the phone to tell me how happy he is that he's hired us. This is a call he does not have to make. It is a call he wants to make because we have made his job easier. He tells me we always seem to get the right products in front of him at the

right time, and that the invoices are easy to understand and easy
for him to pay. I told him we like that comment, especially! He
also said he was pleased Jennifer visited him personally last
month, just to let him know our entire team is at his disposal.

And here's what Gil tells me at the end: He says I must have
the best team in the company and that I must feel lucky to be in
the position I'm in.

Here's how I respond. I thank Gil. I tell him I'm proud of
what our team has been able to do for him, and I tell him he's
right. I say I am delighted and honored to lead you in your efforts.

This story close is more emotive than the repetition close
because it directs the audience to imagine the supporting statements and power sound bite coming to life. This will take some
more work on your part in preparation, and a calmer, friendlier
cadence than the rhythmic repetition close. I believe it also creates the strongest bond with the audience.

In Conclusion, Don't Say "In Conclusion"

Blasphemy again, I know, because it is the delightful and rare
(and always strong) speaker who does not announce the end is
at hand. Most speakers feel compelled to tip us off to what's
coming with the words "in conclusion," but that doesn't make
it right. It's just another crutch for the jumpy speaker to reassure
himself by blurting out something that doesn't help the audience. Or it's just another link in the never-ending cycle of audience abuse that I'd like you to end. It's a tough habit to break.
Exclude the seemingly innocuous "in conclusion," because it

slows down your conclusion and your energy, and worst of all it jars and breaks your connection with the audience. When a speaker says "in conclusion," an unproductive ripple of unrest flows through the audience. Everybody starts to get their stuff together, just when you're building to your power close.

These "in conclusion" speakers would have the same effect by saying, "I'm going to tell you I'm concluding now, so if you want to stop listening to me and my insightful ideas so you can pack up your briefcases and valises. This is a great time to do just that." Resist the urge. Keep "in conclusion" to yourself.

The Ask

After all this work, the speaker is entitled and has earned the right to "ask" the audience for something, in a simple, clear sentence. The audience wants to know what you want from them. Please, don't disappoint. You've earned the right through your power open, the introduction and support of your power sound bite, and the tremendous power close. Now tell the audience what you want from them. Maybe you want specific action, like to buy something from you. Maybe you want them to see things differently or to change their opinion. Maybe you want them to accomplish something for you or do something for themselves. It doesn't matter, but you have the right and (feigned indignation!) the duty, to ask them for something. They expect it, you deserve it.

Let's go back to the power sound bites from chapter 2 and match a strong ask to go along with each one.

Example 1: *You are the best team in the region. You are the ones who will show everyone else how to achieve superior results. I'm delighted and honored to lead you in your efforts.* The ask: *Please work hard at accomplishing these specific actions in the next year. I believe in our team. Please, believe in your own ability to reach your goals. (pause) Thank you!*

Example 2: *When you support my goals for the direction of our marketing efforts you'll be assuring your future, making your customers happy, and putting more money in your wallets.* The ask: *Please approve my marketing plan today. (pause) Thank you!*

Example 3: *Our team has done a great job on the production floor to meet all of our customers' needs, despite a wide variety of obstacles and a lack of support from our colleagues. We will continue to succeed.* The ask: *Please ignore what the sales guys are saying behind our backs. Please pay attention to what counts, our work today. (pause) Thank you!*

Example 4: *The only way you ensure your success in the future is to take time every year to study the changes that software developments are creating on the accounting industry.* The ask: *Please keep your skills sharp, especially your software skills, or you'll fall behind the other guys in the industry. Please put the work in to stay on top. (pause) Thank you!*

The ask should be easy to understand and direct. It should be brief. It should be short, and always a request: "Please." It should be followed by a dramatic pause and then an emphatic, face-up and voice-proud, "thank you." Finish that way and you tell the audience, "It's a great time for you to clap now."

Questions: A Dangerous Minefield Worth the Effort

This is what the pros know about Q&A: It's a huge ally for you. Smart presenters know that the Q&A can help them drive home their power sound bite, as well as provide the right environment for a repeat of the ask. The Q&A period is not only the time for you to provide more facts, it is the time for you to maintain and perhaps increase your connection with the audience.

Most presenters only see the question-and-answer period as a time to answer questions. That glass-half-empty supposition is a mistake and a waste of great opportunities. Questions from the audience should always be treated as another chance to persuade the audience about the value of your PSB and the ask. Let's take a look at the ways in which you can turn the run-of-the-mill Q&A session time into a strong connection time with the audience.

Learn to Love Yes/No Questions

The speaker is throwing away a great opportunity by answering yes/no questions with merely a "yes" or a "no." Yes/no questions give every speaker a chance to launch into the power sound bite, renew the ask or a supporting statement, in addition to sounding definitive and confident. Here's the formula: When you receive a yes/no question, answer one of two ways:

- *Yes, and let me tell you why* . . . (explanation refers back to power sound bite)
- *No, and let me tell you why not* . . . (explanation refers back to power sound bite)

Let's see how this would work in our power sound bite and the ask from the scenario in chapter 2. I've bracketed the reinforcement of the power sound bite.

Audience question 1: *Will everyone be required to learn the new software database, even those who won't have much reason to use it?*

Strong answer: *Yes, and let me tell you why. I want everyone to know how to be able to use it as soon as possible. I want to create an organization where all of us can have access to all of our information about our customers and their orders, instantly. [When everyone knows how to quickly get the information they need, we're making our strong team even stronger: the best team in the region even better.]*

Audience question 2: *Will Jennifer's promotion and job change take effect immediately?*

Strong answer: *No, and let me tell you why not. Jennifer is going to need six weeks to help her replacement, Chad, get a handle on all of her duties. We want to make sure we're moving quickly, but thoughtfully. [We have to make sure we're always taking care of customers and you, our teammates, without missing a beat, as we move forward to meet all of our goals.]*

In both of these circumstances, just "yes" or just "no" would work but would leave a lot of momentum and audience connection on the table. Always be willing to devote the time and energy to answering a yes/no question with a strong tie-in to the power sound bite or the ask.

It's Okay If You Don't Know

Great, experienced, confident speakers look forward to hearing questions from the audience that they cannot answer. Now you will too. Hearing a question you can't answer should bolster your confidence, not create fear. When you hear a question you cannot answer, you have a great chance to reinforce your connection to the audience and demonstrate integrity. It's easy! When you hear a question you can't answer, just say, "I don't know. But I'll find out and get back to you." Make sure you get a card and send an e-mail with the answer the next day. Wow! Not only are you a powerful and sensitive speaker, but you're also a great guy or gal, because you're the type of person who "gets back." We all love someone who "gets back to us." We disdain someone whom we never hear from again. And here's the good news, the reason you should be happy to hear questions. It's only when you don't know the answer that you have a chance to "get back" and be a great individual. You should look forward to not knowing the answer to a question from the audience. It's your key to a powerful extra audience connection.

Many of us are scared by questions we don't have the answer to because of the trauma and scars of school. Did I mention that I got a "D" in trigonometry over thirty years ago? Most presentation situations are far more benign than my schools ever were. Most customers, bosses, and associates don't expect you to know everything. If they do, you've got other professional issues more serious than the skills with which you deliver a presentation.

The audiences I see every week enjoy speakers who admit they don't know the answer to every question they're asked, but are willing to find out. It's a sign of modesty, humility, and a commitment on your part to fulfilling a homework assignment. Not knowing the answer to every question is just fine. Just make sure you always "get back." You need to see the connection in getting back to the person who asked you the question.

Wimps Repeat and Paraphrase Questions

This goes against the grain of what you've heard over the years. Here's my rebuttal to all those who preach that repeating questions is good.

◆ *Repeating the question demonstrates the speaker's sympathy and empathy.*

I think this practice is patronizing, not sympathizing. Audience members do not require your assistance or parental repetition to boost their ideas or questions to your level. Everybody in the room is equal. They don't need your help. They get to ask their questions, you get to respond with your answers.

◆ *Repeating questions shows the speaker striving to understand the audience.*

Many times the repetition of a question just masks the speaker's attempt to stall or buy time. A beat or two of reflection, followed by a strong answer, keeps the speaker in control and focused on the power sound bite.

- ◆ *Repeating the question creates a stronger bond between presenter and audience.*

This technique makes the speaker look weak, as well as patronizing. Why on earth would you want to repeat negative questions from the audience and have negative or challenging words that tear down your presentation come out of your mouth and fill the room? It's passive and defeating, not strong. Let the audience challenge your presentation. Listen without agreeing or disagreeing. Give it that powerful pause and then finally answer the challenging questions with a strong, affirmative response and a return to your power sound bite. All the while, keep your eyes focused, if possible, on the audience member who asked you the negative question. The questioner may not agree with you but should appreciate your respect of the question and your thoughtful answer. That builds a strong bond, much better than merely parroting the negative questions. This is a great opportunity to win over the naysayers in the room. Don't blow it by having their negative words come from your lips. Good presenters know that a strong agenda-based answer to a direct challenge is a great way to keep connecting with the audience. It creates an atmosphere of intensity in the room and healthy friction. It makes the presenter more memorable.

What If You or the Rest of the Audience Can't Hear the Question?

Now, *this* is a great time for all the sympathy/empathy stuff. If the audience can't hear the questions, request that questioners ask them again, louder. Encourage the individuals to bellow out their questions, or have a microphone passed to them. But make sure it is they, not you, repeating the questions. This is another connection builder, especially when you proclaim, "I want to hear the question and I want to make sure everyone else does also. Please ask your question again, just much louder!" This shows you want to connect and that you're not going to usurp their one time in the spotlight by kindly repeating their questions for them. If a question is negative or challenging, so much the better. Harsh questions usually become softer the second or third time they are asked, because the questioner loses conviction at the sound of his or her own voice. They tend to tone down the rough edges the second time around. It works to your favor to dismiss the urge to repeat the question. Instead, have the audience member re-ask the question, several times if necessary.

"That's a Good Question" Is Never a Good Answer

You hear this from a lot of speakers, but that doesn't make it good. When a speaker says, "that's a good question," does that mean all the other questions were moronic, sophomoric, or displayed a complete lack of intellect whatsoever? Or does it mean

the speaker fancies the look of the person who asked this par-
ticular question and is pandering to curry their favor? Neither is
helpful to your professional integrity, so remember: All questions are equal to you, the presenter. None are good, none are
bad. Just answer them all with the same enthusiasm. No apple
polishing, no trashing the other, more mundane, questions.

When you get a "good question," just hold the temptation
to dish out a compliment or to say, "I'm glad you asked that."
Pause, and respond with gusto, returning to your power sound
bite. If you bump into the questioner later in the hall, please sig-
nify one on one that you were glad the person asked the question (not that it was good or great), and that it helped you with
your presentation. That's the type of kind and thoughtful
response which will keep you memorable.

Reap the Benefits of a Good Performance: Accept the Compliment

Make sure you keep all the professional chips you win with a
great presentation. Please, don't throw those chips away with
false modesty or by disagreeing with an audience member who
has taken the time to give you a compliment.

The correct response to "I enjoyed your presentation" is
"thank you," first and foremost, every time. The urge to lock our
thumbs in our belt loops, bow our heads reverentially, cross our
boots in the sand in that slightly embarrassed pose, and say, "Aw
heck, t'warn't nuthin'" after someone tells us we've done a good
job is deeply ingrained in our collective soul. And that John

Wayne/Gary Cooper impersonation is a bad career move. When someone takes the time to compliment you on your insightfulness, your hard work, or your enthusiasm, you should always say "Thank you. Your kind words make me feel good!"

Once you disagree with the person who compliments you ("Oh, I just threw that together. I wish I'd had more time to prepare"), you create an uncomfortable moment. The complimenting person feels trapped and that he has to keep complimenting you. You keep denying it, because you've been trained to say, "Aw heck, t'warn't nuthin'." Eventually the poor person trying to say something nice and positive while increasing his connection to you will get tired and wish he'd never bumped into you. He will make you out to be an insecure wreck, or he may start thinking, "You know, you're right. It really wasn't that great."

False modesty means you're missing a chance to deepen the business relationship. You've worked hard to be great. Now reap the rewards. Say "thank you," then go ahead and ask the person with the compliment about himself: what he does, how he reacted to one or more of your supporting statements. Trade business cards, show off more of your industry knowledge, get a new sales appointment, and increase your business network. It all starts with looking the person in the eye and saying "thank you." If you sense the compliment is sincere, and you can still not bring yourself to say "thank you" first and foremost, then you are insecure and need more help than I can provide in *Presentation S.O.S.* Sometimes, your audience members want to continue the connection with you days and weeks after your presentation. Give them and give yourself the opportunity to enjoy it. It's the payoff you so richly deserve for overcoming the fear and learning to love to stand before an audience.

Action items for your next presentation:
1. Craft and deliver either the repetition or the story power close, giving the audience a full dose of your power sound bite one more time.
2. Make the ask. They're ready for it.
3. Realize that questions are a great time for the reinforcement of your power sound bite and the ask.
4. Never repeat a question or compliment with the words, "good question."
5. Learn to love to say "thank you." It's the key to making your connection with the audience last for days and weeks.

Now, let's put all the lessons from these chapters together in a step-by-step action plan so you will rock their world at your upcoming presentation.

9

You Are Ready to Rock:
The Official Phases of Preparation
for Your Presentation

WHAT YOU WILL LEARN FROM THIS CHAPTER:

- How you're already a better presenter than you were eight chapters ago.
- How to execute three phases to prepare for your presentation.
- How to practice, practice, and practice.

If you've reached this point, you're already a better presenter than when you first opened *Presentation S.O.S.* I say that with confidence even if you disagree with every single tip, every rule, every analogy I've offered. Even if you found nothing illuminating or helpful, you're better off just for devoting this much time and effort to examining the ways to become stronger when you face an audience.

You're developing your own distinct presentation style ideas, your own protocol, and your own foundation, which will give you confidence, whether or not your style includes accepting some or none of my ideas. Your developing presentation strength will chase away those nagging fears of chapter 1. So congratulations! You've studied, worked, and improved, and you will have more confidence next time you're in front of the podium, even if you plan to say "basically" every chance you get!

Now I want to give you a detailed game plan for the development of your presentation as well as a practice schedule. Your goal is to create an order and a discipline to the process of preparing for a presentation, so you'll never feel that "oh my gosh, what am I gonna do?" feeling again, even if you only have a day or two to get ready. Many speakers wait until the last minute to prepare, and it is not because they're laggards. It's because of the natural inclination to delay something when we have no idea where to begin. I'll give you the start, middle, and end of the preparation process, which concludes when the first

words come out of your mouth and you sense an immediate connection with the audience.

Preparation Phase 1: Setting Goals

Take the time to set goals for your presentation. It's such an
intense professional experience—with such great potential
rewards as well as the exposure to criticism—you need to figure
out what you want to get out of it.

Someone is always in charge of co-coordinating your presentation, making sure people show up to listen: your boss, your
banker, your customer, your head of HR. Someone is requesting
that you cough up what you know to others, so that they can be
better off for it. This person may work for you, you may work
for her, you may be colleagues, but someone is organizing this
shebang. It's her party and she's the leader of the rabble who is
bestowing the false dictatorship to you. This is your contact,
your liaison to the group, and you must ask this person for help.
Literally, I want you to ask for help. As soon as you accept the
assignment, ask your contact this question:

*Let's imagine that I've given the perfect presentation you
believe best helps this group. After I'm done, what does the audience know, what does the audience understand, and how is the
audience better off for spending that thirty minutes listening to me?*

This is my first step for every single speaking engagement
and workshop assignment. It's a useful exercise that builds con-

fidence immediately. First, you're bonding quickly with your contact, the leader of the rabble. She will like that you want to create a positive experience for the audience. Second, she will be flattered, and you'll be comfortable in the fact you are asking her advice without pandering to her ego. You need her help to do a good job and she will be glad you asked.

Finally, she will give you direct marching orders. She will tell you exactly what she expects for the audience to proclaim your presentation a big hit. Listen, and if possible take down a note or two. Then, at the end of the conversation, repeat those goals. Once she agrees that you've got it right, ask her if there's anything else you need to accomplish to create a rewarding presentation experience. She'll tell you, and she will be direct. The mystery of "oh my gosh, what do they want me to say?" will be over as soon as you accept the assignment, so you should always ask your "handler" for this advice and counsel. By doing so you're already connecting with at least one member of the audience!

Once you know what the audience is expecting, turn the focus inward. Based on what the audience wants, and who makes up that audience, I'd like you to ask yourself, *"When my presentation is done, how do I expect I will have positively influenced the audience? What will they do differently as a result of the connection I make with them?"*

This is not self-centered, just rational. You, the presenter, have expended energy, time, and effort to give them something. It's reasonable and fair for you to expect something in return. If your presentation is to a prospective customer, you want that person to issue you a purchase order. If it's to a student group, you want to inspire new ideas. If the presentation is to a government body, you want a change in public policy. You should always expect the audience will do something different, however small, because of the time they have spent with you.

You're now in good shape to tackle your power sound bite. With the knowledge of the audience's expectations and what you hope to accomplish, you're ready to create your PSB. Remember to follow the power-sound-bite rules, making sure your "memorable statement":

- is about the audience.
- is direct, strong, and simple.
- is not defensive.
- asks the audience to take new or different actions.

When you've completed presentation preparation Phase 1, you've accomplished a lot. You know what the audience wants, you've determined how you'd like to positively influence the audience, and you have created your memorable power sound bite.

Going through the Phase-1 process makes putting together your upcoming talk much easier. Many of the speakers I work with dive right into the fray, assembling facts and figures without context or meaning. They usually wind up with a deliverable presentation, but one that lacks focus, intensity, or lasting effect. By figuring out what the audience wants, what you want, and how you want to be memorable before you create a single slide, you'll be in confident control of the rest of the preparation process.

Preparation Phase 2: The Nuts and Bolts

This is the heavy-lifting part of the preparation process. But in the end you'll be more efficient, less stressed, and even feeling those tingles of excitement now that you've finished Phase 1. In Phase 2 you'll go through the process of getting all your facts and ideas organized, developing your stories, power open, and power close.

Build your template: If you're up and running on PowerPoint, you'll be able to use the program to build your presentation template. It will take about ten minutes. If you are new to PowerPoint, but know your way around a computer, you should be able to spend sixty to ninety minutes mastering the basics of a very helpful tool and then be ready to build your template. If you don't have PowerPoint and don't want it, and prefer to write things down, you're still in good shape. Get out your pad, note cards, or Royal typewriter and you can build your presentation template as well. Here's how the sixteen slides, note cards, or really bold handwriting on your legal pad will guide you through the rest of the process:

1. My Presentation Action Title
2. My Power Sound Bite
3. Supporting Statement #1
4. Supporting Statement #1: Data/Info Slide

5. Supporting Statement #1: Data/Info Slide
6. Supporting Statement #1: Story Slide
7. Supporting Statement #2
8. Supporting Statement #2: Data/Info Slide
9. Supporting Statement #2: Data/Info Slide
10. Supporting Statement #2: Story Slide
11. Supporting Statement #3
12. Supporting Statement #3: Data/Info Slide
13. Supporting Statement #3: Data/Info Slide
14. Supporting Statement #3: Story Slide
15. My Power Sound Bite
16. My Presentation Action Title

Now you've got your work cut out for you, but you see what you have to do. Complete your first step by creating the supporting statements and the backup you want to provide for each of them. Then, create your stories for each supporting statement. Probably, you'll wind up with sixteen slides, give or take. You may want three or more data/info slides for each supporting statement, or four stories, but create a slide for each one of your three or four stories.

Filling Out Your Presentation: Creating the Audience Connection

The purpose of a template is to allow your thoughts to organize, develop, and flourish. If you lay out this exact template after completing Phase 1, you'll have an easy time (maybe for the first time ever) quickly deciding what you want to say, what order you want to say it in, and what facts, data, and stories you need to back it all up. Follow the steps in chapters 2 and 3 to fill in and develop your supporting statements for your power sound bite and the stories that will make them come alive. Add your data, facts, and additional ideas while maintaining that connection with the audience using the advice of chapters 6 and 7. Finally, if you're going to use PowerPoint, make your slides sticking to the guidelines of chapter 5 (remember: large text, fewer words!).

Completing Phase 2

Save your power open, power close, and the title of your presentation until you have decided on the meat of your presentation. It will be easier, faster, and more fun this way. Your creativity and excitement should be building after you have the bulk of your ideas in place. That's the best time to use your energy to plan your inspirational and riveting open and close. Your power open and your power close may not require slides, but you may just want to leave your PSB up for each one.

Finally, spend some time on your title. In chapter 5 we went through three different title slides: one boring, one average, and one strong. Devote the energy to creating a strong and vibrant title slide. You may only quickly refer to it, if at all, but it is the first thing the audience will see as they file into the room. Let the audience know from the beginning that this isn't just another presentation but a remarkable presentation that they will remember. A strong title slide with insightful text, instead of just a label (i.e., *2006 Marketing Plan*), will get you off on the right foot.

Preparation Phase 3: Practice, Practice, Practice

This is the last step to defeating the fear demon way back in chapter 1. Please, please, practice your presentation, repeatedly. You've just crafted a memorable, insightful, and wonderful presentation . . . perhaps the best you've ever created. Now make sure you understand all the nuances, all of your creation's ebbs and flows. That's the biggest reason to practice: so that you can know what's coming next. This helps you build pace, cadence, and rhythm. It can rescue you in case something goes wrong like a power outage, or computer or projector dying. The coolest cucumbers during a presentation crisis, the ones who leave you in awe when their roof falls in, are the ones who are extremely familiar with every slide, every graph, and every chart of their presentation.

The great ones know they have to practice delivering all these great thoughts and ideas, even though they've come up with them themselves. Here's a practice schedule that works. Even if you can't meet this schedule, try to get in at least two full presentation run-throughs (in a room with the door closed) before you reach the room you'll be speaking in. Practice is what keeps the heart rate manageable, the throat open, and the palms dry come showtime.

Two days before the presentation: Practice does not mean

skimming through the presentation on your computer screen while you're on hold, waiting to place a lunch take-out order. Practice is the process of delivering your presentation from start to finish—in a room by yourself—using the same notes, cards, or papers you will be using during your presentation. It's great if you can have your computer and PowerPoint with you during this practice session, but it's not critical. Hitting your speech three full times forty-eight hours before you face an audience will allow you to become comfortable with your words and presentation order, as well as the delivery of your power sound bite and the telling of your stories. Run through it every time, with your full presentation voice, feeling the power sound bites and seeing the people in your stories.

The night before the presentation: Three more times, with gusto. Try to get this session in before you're too worn out. If you're done by 8:00 p.m. you'll still have enough energy to root for your *Survivor* favorite at tribal council. Be comfortable knowing you have six full practice sessions under your belt. You will not only know the material, you will feel the conviction and weight of all of your statements. You should start to realize you are going to succeed. You'll know you'll be able to connect with audience members and keep all but the least attentive away from the fantasy football draft.

Day of the presentation: One more full run-through in the morning, maybe even at home before you head off to work. This will make the commute pleasant. You should be excited and happy, knowing you are ready.

Just before the presentation: When the computer and projector are set up and you've gone through the slides to make sure they are all in order, take a minute to stand at the podium and practice your power open. If no one is in the room, really belt it out. Even if you can't pull off this final run-through, rest easy. You have practiced and practiced. You know your power sound bite, your supporting statements, and all the data and information on all the slides. You should know by now that you *will* connect with the audience.

Action items for your next presentation:
1. Find out what the audience expects of you.
2. Understand what your goals are.
3. Create your presentation, using the template.
4. Practice, starting two days before showtime.
5. Step to the podium and realize you will be great.

Conclusion

You once had an exhilarating dream. In this dream you were standing before a group of your colleagues, customers, or friends, ready to speak. As you launched into your powerful messages, you saw the audience members on the edge of their seats, clapping and delightedly cheering your insight, poignancy, and brilliance. In this dream you won the audience over, you connected with them. You saw them perhaps even dabbing their eyes from the humor and sensitivity. Now they're patting you on the back as you leave the room, thrusting their business cards into your hands while saying, "Great job. We have to talk about this, I'll call you." And that's when you realize your beautiful dream was real.

This can and will really happen at your next presentation. Your talk will have a riveting effect on the audience. Your power sound bite, stories, power open, power close, and clear command of the room during the Q&A period will give you an executive presence that will cause others to sit up and take notice, and it will give you a confidence you did not know you had.

Congratulations. You are now a speaker who knows how to connect with an audience. Your dream has become a reality.

About the Author

MARK WISKUP is a professional communications coach and the president of Wiskup Communications. He travels the country extensively, working with executives, managers, sales teams, and customer service personnel. He has been a television news journalist and a media production company owner, and holds degrees from UCLA and Northwestern University. He lives in Tampa, Florida, with his wife, Renee. He is proud not only to be the father of two children, but also of the fact that he once served as a driver for Ian Anderson and the rock band Jethro Tull.